EPITAPHS
A Dying Art

Edited by Samuel Fanous

Bodleian Library
UNIVERSITY OF OXFORD

For Geoffrey

First published in 2016 by the Bodleian Library
Broad Street, Oxford OX1 3BG

www.bodleianshop.co.uk

ISBN: 978 1 85124 451 5

Introduction, selection and arrangement © Samuel Fanous, 2016

Cover design by Dot Little at the Bodleian Library
Designed by Dot Little
Typeset by JCS Publishing Services Ltd in 10pt/12pt Adobe Garamond Pro
Printed and bound in Croatia by Zrinski D.D. on 80gsm Munken Premium
Cream

British Library Catalogue in Publishing Data
A CIP record of this publication is available from the British Library

Contents

Introduction

And Rachel died, and was buried on the way to Ephrath, which is
Bethlehem. And Jacob set a pillar upon her grave: that is the pillar of
Rachel's grave unto this day (Genesis 35:19).

Collecting epitaphs, by wandering through graveyards or calling
up tomes in libraries where records abound, remains a satisfying
pastime. Their appeal is as timeless as life itself: how, in death, is life
circumscribed and summarized? After the proverbial three score and
ten years, such a seemingly long time, what does one say by way of
summary in just a few words?

The fact that a summary is necessary is itself noteworthy. For
millennia, where means permitted, it was not enough simply to lay
the body of the deceased in the earth. A tablet, or a marker of some
description was erected and on it, however brief, a fitting recognition
of the deceased. At the conclusion of one of the great biblical love
stories, Jacob erects a pillar, which could still be seen at the time the
story was written, over the tomb of his beloved Rachel, who died in
childbirth. Perhaps it bore an inscription of some sort.

Memorial inscriptions were widespread in ancient civilizations from
Egypt to Sumeria, Greece, Rome and China, as attested by surviving
specimens. In Britain, many survive from the Roman era (first to fifth
centuries). This inscription, until recently in the Ashmolean Museum,
Oxford, is typical:

To the spirits of the departed and to Vivius Marcianus, centurion of
the Second Legion Augusta, Januaria Martina his most devoted wife
set up this memorial.

Anglo-Saxon stone memorials, which date from the late seventh century onwards, sometimes took the form of requests for prayer:

> Tunwine put up this cross in memory of his lord [or son] Torhtred.
> Pray for his soul.

In the middle ages, churchyards contained few tombstones. Most of the dead were simply interred in the ground, perhaps with a temporary marker, usually made from wood. Initially only saints and the clergy were buried within the church building, the gravestones of the latter marked with a simple Latin inscription and sometimes an elongated cross. From the thirteenth century onwards the laity, primarily knights, came to be buried within churches. The earliest surviving epitaph in English is thought to be on Emma, the wife of Fulk (c. 1300) and is found in Stow Minster, Lincolnshire:

> Alle men that bere lif
> prai for Emma was Fulk wif

After the Reformation, tombstones and other memorials multiplied, reflecting both increasing prosperity across society and a new sense of individual identity. The wealthy erected ever more elaborate monuments, perhaps rivalling medieval chantry chapels, until in some cases they were out of proportion with the rest of the fabric of the church. By the time John Weever produced the first collection of epitaphs in 1631, the decoration of tombs had so advanced that he could complain:

> If one should seriously survey the tombs erected in these our days, and examine the particulars of the personages wrought upon their tombs, he may easily discern the vanity of our minds, veiled under our fantastic habits and attires, which, in time to come, will be rather provocations to vice, than incitations to virtue; and so the temple of God shall become a school house of the monstrous habits and attires of our present age ... And, which is worse, they garnish their

Tombes, now adays, with the pictures of naked men and women; raising out of the dust and bringing unto the Church, the memories of the heathen gods and goddesses, with all their whirligigs.

It was the Reformation that made possible this trend, as Weever himself attests:

Certain persons, of every county, were put in authority to pull down, and cast out of all churches, roods [crucifixes], graven images [statues], shrines with their relics, to which the ignorant people came flocking in adoration. Or anything else which (punctually) tended to idolatry and superstition.

In place of such screens and saints' statues secular memorials were erected to those whose social position or civic achievements merited memorialization. Westminster Abbey, once a thriving Benedictine house, is perhaps the most obvious example of this trend. While it served as a burial place for some kings before the Reformation, it and later St Paul's Cathedral became national shrines and sculptural showpieces. By the seventeenth century, the stone memorial was widely used in churchyards. The first upright tombstones in the New World are to passengers on the Mayflower.

Over the centuries the contents and mode of epitaphs, and the mood they conveyed, evolved. Medieval memorials are generally short and often contain prayers for the souls of the deceased or admonitions to the onlooker to pray for them. With their iconography of death (carved skulls, bones, hour-glasses, scythes, mort bells) and their warnings to prepare for the terrible hour, many seventeenth- and eighteenth-century tombstones serve to reprove the living. Yet this was also the era of the great flowering of epitaphs and left us some of the most entertaining, discursive, and light-hearted, not to mention eloquent, memorial inscriptions. By the nineteenth century, the symbols of death were generally replaced by high-minded moralization, sentimentality, or religious fervour, and with them symbols of the resurrection. Victorian epitaphs can be verbose and speak of the relief of death from the toils of life, of the rewards that await the faithful in the life to come, or of the innocence of children who return to their maker. Many are concerned with consoling the bereaved and seem to have been written in a moment of intense grief.

Twentieth-century epitaphs tend towards a record of the bare facts: names and dates, perhaps with a biblical phrase or a short sentiment. By comparison with earlier centuries, one might be forgiven for thinking that the art of the epitaph was dead. While this trend is undeniable, there a few examples to the contrary such as C.S. Lewis' epitaph on his wife Joy Davidman and Spike Milligan's own inscription. In the 1920s and 1930s, American celebrities were invited by magazines to suggest their own epitaphs, resulting in pithy, playful phrases. Similar sentiments made their way onto tombstones later in the century; some are recorded in Chapter 5.

Epitaphs are written for a variety of purposes: to record relevant facts of the life or death of the deceased; express sentiment; record piety or cynicism; console the bereaved; affirm or deny belief in the afterlife; praise or denounce the dead as well as those in their circle; promote the work of the deceased; or exhort the living. Those employing excessive puns suggest they were written as much if not more in self-admiration than in commemoration, such as this epitaph said to have been in Peterborough Cathedral on one Sir Richard Worme (d. 1589):

> Does Worm eat Worme? Knight Worme this truth confirms,
> For here, with worms, lies Worme, a dish for worms.
> Does worm eat Worme? sure Worme will this deny,
> For Worme with worms, a dish for worms don't lie.
> 'Tis so, and 'tis not so, for free from worms
> 'Tis certain Worme is blest without his worms.

Some twentieth-century epitaphs seem to embody a new purpose: entertainment, especially through humour. While this may seem appropriate for a comic actor like Jack Lemmon (p. 110), intended humour can easily transgress into the seemingly inappropriate or plain bad taste, and beyond into the appalling (p. 111).

A vast library of works on epitaphs has been published: from a surprising number of anthologies to essays on the subject, notably by William Wordsworth and Samuel Johnson, as well as many scholarly articles and books. There are even volumes of suggested epitaphs for monumental masons and sculptors, a tradition which stretches back to John Bowden's *The Epitaph Writer, Consisting of Six Hundred Original Epitaphs, Moral, Admonitory, Humorous and Satirical ... Chiefly Designed for Those Who Wish to Write or Engrave Inscriptions on Tombstones* (1791). In addition to the antiquarian collections of epitaphs, county and parish histories are a rich source for the epitaph hunter.

While there can be no substitute for visiting cemeteries, the internet has changed the landscape of epitaphs by providing a vast number of images of tombstones from cemeteries round the world, making it possible to transcribe these texts from some distance (though beware the fakes, often the product of poor photo-editing skills and almost always purveying absurdly improbable contents). These images have been posted online by churches (Westminster Abbey), cemeteries (Kensal Green), various bodies (National Maritime Museum), specialist websites (findagrave.com, www.geograph.org.uk), as well as by an army of individual visitors to cemeteries or memorial sites. A good number of the inscriptions in this book have been transcribed from photographs from these and other internet sources. Others are taken from printed and digital sources listed in the Bibliography as well as from visits to graveyards.

Stone seems lasting but is in fact fugitive. The fine words incised on lapidary monuments are only a few millimetres deep, so that in many instances the elements erode the mason's marks in just a few short decades. Indoors, those on church floors are trampled on and wear out. This makes it necessary to rely on records made when the stones were legible. Not all compilers in previous centuries were guided by the same standards. Some reproduce epitaphs with scant information about the names of individuals, their dates, or sometimes even the place. The same epitaph sometimes appears in a variety of forms, according to the editor. And because often the stones have long vanished, it becomes difficult to rely on many of these 'recycled' epitaphs, especially when there are unaccompanied by provenance. I have tried to sift the unlikely from the probable through a combination of the reliability of sources, attendant specificity (name, place, date), as well as plausibility. I have retained a small number of untraceable epitaphs because of their intrinsic value and have noted these with a caveat.

While some of the epitaphs in this book are from tombstones, others are from memorial inscriptions, sometimes composed and erected centuries after the death. Many of the war dead are commemorated collectively on memorial plaques, a few of which have been included. A number are from monuments on walls near to the place of burial. The English-speaking world has produced epitaphs of astonishing variety and eccentricity; nevertheless, a few in this volume are translations from ancient and modern languages. While the style and contents of epitaphs may be culturally conditioned, the sentiments expressed in them are surprisingly common across the centuries. This book therefore ranges quite widely, from ancient Greece to the twenty-first century. The result may seem disparate and incongruous; yet recognizable themes emerge, common to the human condition across time and space.

To give some structure to this highly subjective assemblance, I have arranged the entries thematically and within chapters I have tried further to group epitaphs, even if somewhat arbitrarily. Numerous epitaphs could easily fit in more than one chapter. Rather than peppering the text with excessive prose by way of context, I have kept the commentary to a minimum so as to allow the epitaphs to speak for themselves.

There is a great tradition of literary epitaphs in English, written while the individual was alive and generally not intended for actual use. Composed in the style of an epitaph, they vary in mood from solemnity to mirth, jest, or invective, and constitute a genre which flourished in the eighteenth and nineteenth centuries. I have assembled a small collection of them in Chapter 7.

Where possible, I have transcribed the epitaphs retaining spelling, line breaks, and capitalization, but not italicization (especially rife in eighteenth-century inscriptions) or relative sizes. I have not always included the entire text of an epitaph and have tried to indicate this in the headnote. This is not a scholarly work so accordingly I have not cited the reference of every entry, but have provided in the Bibliography a list of sources consulted.

Epitaphs retain their power to move us. In the record of their struggles, joys, tragedies, and triumphs we recognize our own experiences and the essential elements that characterize human nature across the spans of time and culture. While each epitaph confirms an individual life and death, collectively they constitute a *speculum*, a mirror of humanity, writ in stone.

In compiling this book, I have been assisted at the Bodleian Library by Chris Hargreaves who with unfailing cheer delivered volume after volume. Janet Phillips gave advice throughout in editing and shaping this selection. Deborah Susman and Emily Brand produced this book with customary efficiency and speed. Nicholas Stogdon and Henrietta Leyser read a draft of this introduction and made helpful comments. My principle debt, however, is to the many compilers of epitaphs over the centuries. Their efforts have been greatly aided by the many visitors to churchyards and cemeteries who have posted images of tombstones and memorials online, continuing an engaging and worthwhile tradition. Any errors are of course my own.

Chapter 1

Long Life,
Love, & Friendship

St Bartholemew, Brightwell Baldwin, Oxfordshire.

STEPHEN RUMBOLD
Born Feb 1582
Died March the 4 1687

He liv'd one hundred and five
Sanguine and strong
An hundred and five
You do not live so long

St Clement, Leigh on Sea, Essex.

HERE LIES THE BODY OF MARY ELLIS,
DAUGHTER OF THOMAS AND LYDIA ELLIS
OF THIS PARISH
SHE WAS A VIRGIN OF VIRTUOUS COURAGE
AND VERY PROMISING HOPE.
AND DIED ON THE 3RD OF JUNE, 1609
AGED ONE HUNDRED AND NINETEEN

Said to have been in St Andrew, Shifnal, Shropshire.

August 7th, 1776,
Mary Yates, of Shifnall. Aged 128.

She lived many years on the bounty of
Sir Harry and Lady Bridgeman.
She walked to London
just after the Fire, in 1666.
She was hearty and strong at 120 years; and
married a third husband at ninety two.

All Saints, Northampton, Northamptonshire.

Here under lyeth
JOHN BAILES born in this

Town he was above 126
years old & had his hearing
Sight and Memory to ye last
He lived in 3 Centurys
& was buried the 14th of Apr
1706.

Arlington, Massachusetts, on Samuel Whittemore (1696–1793), the oldest known combatant in the American Revolutionary War. He died aged 96 (not 98, as his stone says).

NEAR THIS SPOT
SAMUEL WHITTEMORE
THEN 80 YEARS OLD,
KILLED THREE BRITISH SOLDIERS
APRIL 19, 1775
HE WAS BAYONETED
BEATEN AND LEFT FOR DEAD,
BUT RECOVERED AND LIVED TO BE 98 YEARS OF AGE.

St Bartholemew, Longnor, Staffordshire. A note on the reverse of the stone explains that this is a copy created in 1903 of the original decaying stone.

In Memory of William BILLINGE, who
was born in a Cornfield at Fawfieldhead in
this Parish in the Year 1679. At the age of
23 Years he enlisted into his Majesty's Service
under Sir George Rooke and was at the taking
of the Fortress of Gibraltar in 1704. He afterwards served under the Duke of Marlborough at
the ever Memorable Battle of Ramillies,
fought on the 23rd May 1706 where he
was wounded by a musket shot in the thigh.
He afterwards returned to his native country and
with manly courage defended his Sovereigns

rights at the Rebellion in 1715 and 1745. He
died with a space of 150 yards of where
he was born and was interred here the 30
January 1791 aged 112 years.

Billeted by Death I quartered here remain.
When the trumpet sounds I'll rise and march again.

Vernon, Vermont.

EBENEZER SCOTT,
1826, age 83
Grandfather
The first white male born in Bernardston,
Mass. Was taken with his mother and two brothers
By the Indians, carried to Quebec, sold to the
French when he was 8 years old. Returned to his
Father. Served in the Revolution – drew a pension.

Royal Chelsea Hospital, London.

Here Lies WILLIAM HISELAND
A Veteran if ever Soldier was
Who merited well a Pension
If Long Service be a Merit
Having served upwards of the Days of Man
Antient but not Superannuated
Engaged in a series of Wars Civil as well as Foreign
Yet not maimed or worn out by either
His Complexion was fresh & florid
His Health hale & hearty
His Memory exact & ready
In Stature He exceeded the Military size
In Strength He surpassed the prime of Youth
and What rendered his Age Still more Patriarchal

When above one Hundred Years Old
He took unto him a Wife

Read Fellow Soldiers and Reflect
That there is a Spiritual Warfare
As well as a Warfare Temporal
Born vj of August 1620 Died vij of Feb. 1732 Aged 112

St Nicholas, Brighton, East Sussex.

In memory of
PHOEBE HESSEL
who was born at Stepney in the year 1713.
She served for many Years
as a private Soldier in the 5th Regt of Foot
in different parts of Europe
and in the Year 1745 fought under the command
of the DUKE of CUMBERLAND
at the Battle of Fontenoy
where she received a Bayonet wound in her Arm.
Her long life which commenced in the time of
QUEEN ANNE
extended to the reign of
GEORGE IV
by whose munificence she received comfort
and support in her latter Years.
She died at Brighton where she had long resided,
December, 12th 1821. Aged 108 years.

**St John the Baptist, Burford, Oxfordshire, by Elizabeth, Lady Tanfield on her
husband, Sir Lawrence Tanfield (1551–1625).**

Here shadow lie
Whil'st life is sadd,
Still hopes to die
To him she hadd

In bliss is hee,
Whom I lov'd best
Thrise happie shee
With him to rest.

So shall I be
With him I loved
And hee with mee
And both us blessed

Love made me Poet
And this I writt,
My harte did doe yt
And not my witt.

St Mary, Thornbury, Gloucestershire.

In memory of
THOMAS RIDDIFORD
Who died November 19th 1840
Aged 54 years.

Silent grave to thee I trust
this precious pearl of worthy dust
Keep it safe O sacred tomb
until a wife shall ask for room

Old Hill Burying Ground, Newburyport, Massachusetts (partial).

The Remembrance of
DEAN RICHARD SMITH & his Wife ABIGAIL
who lived together fifty three years
in an exemplary manner,
& died Octr. 1806
within five days of each other
in the 79th year of their age

Old Hill Burying Ground, Newburyport, Massachusetts.

In memory of
EDMUND MORSE & MARY his wife
He died May 22,
She the 14, 1790
Each in their 83 year.

Death can not disjoin whom Christ has joind in love
Life leads to death and death to life above

St Mary, Whitby, North Yorkshire.

HERE LIE THE BODIES OF FRANCIS HUNTRODDS AND
MARY HIS WIFE WHO WERE BORN ON THE SAME
DAY OF THE WEEK, MONTH AND YEAR (VIZ) SEPTR YE 19TH
1600, MARRY'D ON THE DAY OF THEIR BIRTH AND AFTER HAVING
HAD 12 CHILDREN BORN TO THEM DIED AGED 80 YEARS
ON THE SAME DAY OF THE YEAR THEY WERE BORN, SEPTEMBER YE
19TH 1680 THE ONE NOT ABOVE FIVE HOURS BEFORE YE OTHER.

HUSBAND AND WIFE THAT DID TWELVE CHILDREN BEAR,
DY'D THE SAME DAY; ALIKE BOTH AGED WERE.
BOUT 80 YEARS THEY LIV'D, FIVE HOURS DID PART,
(EV'N ON THE MARRIAGE DAY) EACH TENDER HEART
SO FIT A MATCH, SURELY COULD NEVER BE;
BOTH, IN THEIR LIVES, AND IN THEIR DEATHS AGREE.

Said to have been in All Saints, Bakewell, Derbyshire (partial).

Know, posterity, that on the 8th of April in the year of Grace, 1737, the
rambling remains of the above said John Dale were, in the 86th yeare of his
pilgrimage, laid upon his two wives.

This thing in life might raise some jealousy,
Here all three lie together lovingly,

But from embraces here no pleasure flows,
Alike are here all human joys and woes;

Here Sarah's chiding John no longer hears,
And old John's rambling Sarah no more fears;
A period's come to all their toilsome lives,
The good man's quiet; still are both his wives.

St Augustine of Canterbury, Birdbrook, Essex.

MARTHA BLEWITT,
of the Swan Inn at Baythorn-End,
of this Parish,
buried May 7th, 1681
was the wife of nine Husbands successively
but the ninth outlived her.
The Text to her Funeral Sermon was:
'Last of all the Woman died also.'

ROBERT HOGAN,
Of this Parish
Was the Husband of Seven Wives successively
He married Ann Livermore his seventh Wife
January 1st 1739

St Giles, Bowes, Durham.

The Lover's Tragedy

ROGER WRIGHTSON JUN. & MARTHA RAILTON
both of Bowes, buried in one grave.
He died of a fever & upon Tolling his passing bell she cried out,
'My heart is broke' and in a few hours Expired thro love.
March 15 1714–15.

Dorchester Abbey, Oxfordshire, on a victim to marital infidelity.

Reader!
If thou has a heart fam'd for
Tenderness and Pity, Contemplate this Spot.
In which are deposited the Remains
Of a Young Lady, whose artless Beauty,
Innocence of Mind and gentle Manners,
Once obtained her the Love and
Esteem of all who knew her, But when
Nerves were too delicately spun to
Bear the rude Shakes and Jostlings
Which we meet with in the transitory
World, Nature gave way; She sunk
And died a Martyr to Excessive Sensibility.
MRS SARAH FLETCHER
Wife of Captain FLETCHER,
Departed this Life at the Village
Of Clifton, on the 7 of June 1799.
In the 29 Year of her Age.
May her Soul meet that Peace in
Heaven which this Earth denied her.

St Vérand, Rhone, France, on Harriet Mill (d. 1859), by her husband, John Stuart Mill.

Were there but a few hearts and intellects like hers this earth would already become the hoped-for heaven.

Crathie, Aberdeenshire, on Queen Victoria's gillie (1826–83).

THIS STONE IS ERECTED
IN AFFECTIONATE
AND GRATEFUL MEMORY OF
JOHN BROWN
THE DEVOTED AND FAITHFUL

PERSONAL ATTENDANT
AND BELOVED FRIEND
OF QUEEN VICTORIA
IN WHOSE SERVICE HE HAD BEEN
FOR 34 YEARS.

BORN CRATHIENAIRD DECEMBER 8TH 1826
DIED WINDSOR CASTLE 27TH MARCH 1883

"THAT FRIEND ON WHOSE FIDELITY YOU COUNT,
THAT FRIEND GIVEN YOU BY CIRCUMSTANCES
OVER WHICH YOU HAVE NO CONTROL, WAS
GOD'S OWN GIFT"

Gonville and Caius, Cambridge, on Thomas Legge, warden, with reference to his friend John Gostlin. The second inscription appears below the representation of two hands holding a flaming heart (tr. from Latin).

Thomas Legge,
Doctor of Laws,
formerly warden of this college,
died in the year of our Lord,
1607, the 12th day of July,
in the 72d year of his age.

Love joined them living. So may the earth join them in their burial.
O Legge, Gostlin's heart you have still with you.

English Cemetery, Rome. Trelawny purchased two graves side by side for Percy Shelley and himself, inscribing Shelley's four-line epitaph on his own tombstone. However, it is thought that Shelley's 'friend' in the poem is Edward Williams, who perished with him in the boating accident and whose body was also washed up on the beach at Viareggio.

EDWARD J. TRELAWNY
DIED IN ENGLAND AUGUST 13TH 1881
AGED 88

THESE ARE TWO FRIENDS WHOSE LIVES WERE UNDIVIDED,
SO LET THEIR MEMORY BE. NOW THEY HAVE GLIDED
UNDER THE GRAVE; LET NOT THEIR BONES BE PARTED.
FOR THEIR TWO HEARTS IN LIFE WERE SINGLE HEARTED.

**St Mary Magdalene, Launceston, Cornwall, on the cenotaph of
Granville Piper (d. 1717) and Richard Wise (d. 1726),
both buried at Bath (tr. from Latin, partial).**

The Empty Tomb of Granville Pyper, Esquire, and Richard Wise,
gentleman, formerly Alderman of this Town, whose mortal remains
are lying at Bath in the County of Somerset.
As they had in life been of one mind and most closely associated
together, so now after death these equally true hearted of friends
are not divided.
The former when much urged to seek his health at Bath, consented.
He died there 16th April in the year of our Lord, 1717, in the 38th year
of his age. The latter dying at Launceston on the 27th July, in the year
of our Lord, 1726, aged 64 wished that his ashes should be deposited
at Bath near those of his most loving and dearest Master.

**Hereford Cathedral, Herefordshire, on Herbert Croft, bishop of Hereford,
buried next to George Benson, dean of Hereford Cathedral (1692). Two clasped
hands engraved in stone join the two memorials. Benson's tombstone concludes
with the second inscription (tr. from Latin, partial).**

Here are deposited the remains of
Herbert Croft of Croft,
bishop of Hereford,
who died 18 May 1691,
the 88th year of his age,
in life united.

In death not divided

Westminster Abbey, London, on Mary Kendall (1607–1709/10) (partial).

… that close Union & Friendship,
In which she liv'd, with
the Lady CATHARINE JONES;
And, in testimony of which she desir'd
That even their Ashes, after Death,
Might not be divided:
And therefore, order'd her Selfe
Here to be interr'd
Where, She knew, that Excellent Lady
Design'd one day, to rest,
Near the Grave of her Belov'd
And Religious Mother
ELIZABETH Countess of RANELLAGH.

Woodlawn Cemetery, Elmira, New York, on Olivia Susan Clemens, adapted by Mark Twain, her father, from a poem by Robert Richardson (partial).

Warm summer sun, shine kindly here;
southern wind, blow softly here;
Green sod above, lie light, lie light –
Good-night, dear heart, good-night, good-night.

Memorial Garden, NAACP, Baltimore, Maryland.

HERE LIE THE ASHES OF DOROTHY PARKER
(1893–1967)
HUMORIST, WRITER, CRITIC.
DEFENDER OF HUMAN AND CIVIL RIGHTS.
FOR HER EPITAPH SHE SUGGESTED
'EXCUSE MY DUST'.
THIS MEMORIAL GARDEN IS DEDICATED TO HER NOBLE
SPIRIT WHICH CELEBRATED THE ONENESS OF HUMANKIND,
AND TO THE BONDS OF EVERLASTING FRIENDSHIP BETWEEN
BLACK AND JEWISH PEOPLE.

Lincoln Cathedral, Lincolnshire.

Here lyeth the body of
MICHAEL HONEYWOOD, D.D.
Who was grandchild, and one of the
Three hundred and sixty-seven persons,
That MARY the wife of ROBERT HONEYWOOD, Esq.
Did see before she died,
Lawfully descended from her,
viz.
Sixteen of her own body, 114 grand children,
288 of the third generation, and 9 of the fourth.
MRS. HONEYWOOD
Died in the year 1605,
And in the 78th year of her age.

Conwy, Conwy County Borough, Wales.

HERE LYETH YE BODYE

OF NICH: HOOKES OF

CONWAY, GEN., WHO

WAS YE 41ST CHILD

OF HIS FATHER WILLIAM

HOOKES ESQR. BY ALICE

HIS WIFE, AND YE FATHER

OF 27 CHILDREN, WHO

DYED YE 20TH DAY OF MARCH

1637.N.B. THIS STONE WAS REV

IVED IN YE YEAR 1720

ATT YE CHARGE OF JOHN

St Mary the Virgin, Saffron Walden, Essex.

To the memory of
Richard Ward Spicer
Born May 13th 1789, Died June 25th 1853.
Dudley Adcock Spicer
Wife of the above,
Born Decr. 28th 1790, Died Septr. 15th 1852.
Also of their children,
Matthew W. Spicer Born Septr. 28. 1812 Died May 3. 1852
Sarah W. Spicer Born Feby. 26. 1814 Died June 5. 1814
Richard Spicer Born Novr. 14. 1815 Died June 15. 1830
Dudley Spicer Born July 20. 1818 Died June 26. 1827
Harriett Spicer Born Augt. 10. 1820 Died Feby. 7. 1855
Sarah Spicer Born May 6. 1822 Died Mar. 10. 1823
William Spicer Born Feby. 21. 1824 Died Septr. 9. 1824
George S. Spicer Born Septr. 21. 1825 Died Decr. 31. 1844
Susannah Spicer Born May 30. 1827 Died Octr. 7. 1838
Richard Spicer Born Octr. 30. 1830 Died May 4. 1833
Dudley Spicer Born June 13. 1832 Died May 1. 1833
Also Jane Wife of Matthew Spicer,
And Daughter of Wm. Low of this Town,
Who Died Octr. 13th 1852 Aged 37.

Chapter 2

Occupations & Professions

St Petrock, Lydford, Devonshire.

Here lies, in a horizontal position,
the outside case of
George Routleigh, Watchmaker,
whose abilities in that line were an honour to his
profession.
Integrity was the mainspring, and prudence the regulator
of all the actions of his life;
Humane, generous, and liberal, his hand never stopped
till he had relieved distress:
So nicely regulated was his movements,
that he never went wrong,
except when set a-going
by people who did not know his key:
Even then he was easily set right again.
He had the art of disposing of his Time,
so well,
That his hours glided away in one
continual round of pleasure and delight,
Till an unlucky moment put a period to his existence.
He departed this life November 14, 1802,
aged 57, wound up,
in hopes of being taken in hand by his Maker:
and of being thoroughly cleaned, repaired, and set a-going
for the world to come.

Westminster Abbey, London on George Graham (d. 1679) (partial).

HERE LIES ...

THE BODY OF

GEORGE GRAHAM OF LONDON

WATCHMAKER AND F.R.S.

WHOSE CURIOUS INVENTIONS

DO HONOUR TO YE BRITISH GENIUS

24

WHOSE ACCURATE PERFORMANCES
ARE YE STANDARD OF MECHANIC SKILL.
HE DIED YE XVI OF NOVEMBER MDCCLI
IN THE LXXVIII YEAR OF HIS AGE.

St Andrew, Buckland Monachorum, Devon, St Britius, Brize Norton, Oxfordshire and numerous others, in slightly different forms (partial).

My sledge and hammer both declin'd.
My bellows too have lost their wind
My fire's extinct my coals decay'd
And in the dust my vice is laid,
My coal are spent, my iron is gone,
My nails are drove, my work is done.

St Mary, Sarnesfield, Herefordshire, on John Abel (1577–1674, partial), appointed King's Carpenter to Charles I during the Civil War. Among his many achievements, he designed and built Snaresfield Church.

This craggy stone a covering is for an Architect's bed
That lofty buildings rais'd high yet now lays low his head
His line and rules so death concludes are locked up in stone
Build they who list or they who wist for he can build no more
His house of clay could hold no longer
May Heaven's joy build him a stronger

Winslow, Maine.

Here lies the body of Richard Thomas
An inglishman by birth
A Whig of '76
By occupation a cooper
Now food for worms.

Like an old rum puncheon whose
Staves are all marked, numbered and shooked

25

He will be raised again and finished
By his creator.

He died Sept. 28, 1824. Aged 75.

The Garden Museum, Lambeth, London, in the deconsecrated church of St Mary, on John Tradescant, the Elder (d. 1638) and Younger (d. 1662). The 'sone' is John the Younger's son, also John, who died at the age of 19.

Know stranger as thou pass, beneath this stone
Lye John Tradescant grandsire, father, sone
The last died in his spring, the other two
Lived till they had travelled art and nature thro'
By their choice collections may appear
Of what is rare in land in sea and air
Whilst they (as Homer's Iliad in a nut)
A world of wonders in one closet shut
These famous Antiquarians that had been
Both gardeners to the Rose and Lily Queen
Transplanted now themselves, sleep here, and when
Angels shall with their trumpets waken men
And fire shall purge the world, these hence shall rise
And change this garden for a Paradise.

Beckenham Cemetery, London. When all attempts failed to counteract huge cracks in the walls of Winchester Cathedral in the early twentieth century, William Walker, a deep-sea diver, worked underwater every day for six years placing bags of concrete. A diver in a diving bell is engraved above the following inscription.

WILLIAM WALKER

M.V.O.

1869–1918

The diver who with
His own hands saved
Winchester Cathedral

St Mary the Virgin, Chipping Norton, Oxfordshire.

Here
lieth the Body of
PHILLIS Wife of
JOHN HUMPHREYS
Rat Catcher
who has Lodged
in many a Town
and Traveled far & near
in Age and death
She is struck down
To her last lodging here
who died June XII 1763
Aged 58

Ripon Cathedral, North Yorkshire.

Here lies poor
but honest Bryan Tunstall;
he was
a most expert angler,
until
Death, envious of his Merit,
threw out his line
hook'd him and
landed him here
the 21st day of April,
1790

Kells, Dumfries and Galloway, Scotland, erected by Capt. John Gordon on his gamekeeper, John Murray, who died in 1777 after 46 years' service. The tombstone shows in relief a gun, powder-flask, fishing rod, and game bird.

Ah, John, what changes since I saw thee last;
Thy fishing and thy shooting days are past,

Bagpipes and hautboys thou canst sound no more;
Thy nods, grimaces, winks and pranks are o'er.
Thy harmless, queerish, incoherent talk.
Thy wild vivacity, and trudging walk
Will soon be quite forgot; thy joys on earth
A snuff, a glass, riddles and mirth
Be vanish'd all, yet blest I hope thou art,
For in thy station weel thou play'st thy part.

Recorded as being in Christ Church, Bristol.

Here lie Tho. Turar, and Mary, his wife. He was twice Master of the
Company of Bakers, and twice Churchwarden of this parish.
He died March 6, 1654. She died May 8th, 1643.

Like to the baker's oven is the grave,
Wherein the bodyes of the faithful have
A setting in, and where they do remain
In hopes to rise, and to be drawn again;
Blessed are they who in the Lord are dead,
Though set like dough, they shall be drawn like bread.

**St Peter, Folkington, Sussex. The headstone is surmounted by a relief depicting
a cooking pot with lid, framing the words 'In fondest memory', surrounded by
vegetable, fruit, and branches bearing small fruit.**

ELIZABETH DAVID

C.B.E.

20 Dec. 1913 – 22 May 1992

Daughter of Rupert Gwynne M.P.
& the Hon. Stella Gwynne
of Wootton Manor, Folkington
Her books on cookery brought joy
And enlightenment to food-lovers
All over the world.

St Peter, Stockbridge, Hampshire.

In memory of
JOHN BUCKETT
many years landlord of the King's head Inn,
in this Borough
who departed this life November 25, 1802
Aged 67 Years.

And is, alas! poor Bucket gone?
Farewell, convivial, honest John.
Oft at the well, by fatal stroke,
Buckets, like pitchers, must be broke.
In this same motley shifting scene,
How various have thy fortunes been!
Now lifted high, now sinking low.
Today thy brim would overflow,
Thy bounty then would all supply
To fill and drink, and leave thee dry;
To-morrow sunk as in a well
Content, unseen, with truth to dwell:
But high or low, or wet or dry,
No rotten stave could malice spy
Then rise, immortal Buckett, rise,
And claim thy station in the skies;
'Twixt Amphora and Pisces shine
Still guarding Stockbridge with thy sign.

Gloucester Cathedral, Gloucestershire, on Samuel Bridger (d. 1650).

Receiver of this College Rents, he paid
His Debt to Nature, and beneath he's laid
To rest, until his summons to remove,
At the last Audit, to the Choir above.

Holy Trinity, Ratcliffe on Soar, Nottinghamshire, on Robert Smith (d. 1782), aged 82.

Fifty-five years it was, and something more,
Clerk of this parish he the office bore,
And in that space, 'tis awful to declare,
Two generations buried by him were.

St Mary, Ottery, Devon. The verse is adapted from Henry Wadsworth Londfellow's 'The Village Blacksmith'.

IN LOVING MEMORY OF
GEORGE GODFREY
BORN OCTOBER 25TH 1834
DIED MAY 5TH 1917

FOR SIXTY YEARS HE DAILY RANG
THE CHURCH BELLS, AND KEPT THE
TOWN CLOCK TO TIME.
TOILING, REJOICING, SORROWING,
ONWARD THROUGH LIFE HE GOES;
EACH MORNING SEES SOME TASK BEGUN,
EACH EVENING SEES ITS CLOSE
LIFE'S PEAL WELL RUNG, NOW COMES REST.

Palgrave, Suffolk. The tombstone depicts a wagon drawn by three pairs of horses.

In Memory of
JOHN CATCHPOLE
Who died 16 June 1787
Aged 75 years

My Horses have done Running.
My Waggon is Decayed.
And now in the Dust my Body is layd
My whip is worn out and my work it is done
And now I'm brought here to my last home.

**Alloa, Clackmannanshire, Scotland, on James McIsack,
a bookseller (d. 1834), aged 66.**

For all the books I've bound
Here now with valley clods,
In sheets I'm rotting under ground,
Death makes as mighty odds!

Waiting the final dawn
Mine ashes here are laid;
Life's labour's o'er, and I'm withdrawn,
Here have I found my bed.

St Michael, Coventry, West Midlands.

Here lie inter'd
the mortal remains of
John Hulme,
Printer
who, like an old worn-out type,
by frequent use, reposes in the grave
But not without a hope that
at some future time he might be
cast in the mould of righteousness
And safely locked up in the blissful chase of immortality
He was distributed from the board of life
on the 9th day of Sept. 1827
regretted by his employers
and
respected by his fellow artists

**Merton College, Oxford (tr. from Latin). Bearing the founder's name from 1604,
the Bodleian continued to be known by 'The Public Library' for some years.**

TO THE MEMORY OF
SIR THOMAS BODLEY
FOUNDER OF THE PUBLIC LIBRARY
DIED 28 JAN. 1612

The Garden Museum, Lambeth, London, in the deconsecrated church of St Mary, on Elias Ashmole (1617–92) (tr. From Latin, partial).

He died on 18 May 1692
aged of 76
But as long as the Ashmolean Museum at Oxford endures,
he will never die

St Leonard, Landulph, Cornwall, on a schoolmaster, said to have been engraved by himself.

A MEMORIALL
Here underneath One buri'd was
Which kept a Schooll at Painter's Cross
Wherein his dayes Ŧ Yeares were Spent
Not for much gaine, yet with content
This Parish was hee did live in
His Place therein was Stockadon
Hee kept his Church ± all things neat
And when therein Here was his Seat
GOD send you then Another such
Your Children well his lawes to teach
To him therefore that craves his name
This stone henceforth doth show ye same
Alexander Moone, Objit
Anno Dom'i 1774
Aged Years

Said to have been in the Rolls Chapel, London, demolished 1895, on Sir John Strange, judge.

Here lies an honest lawyer, –
That is Strange

Tweedsmuir, Peeblesshire, Scotland, on Edward Aitchenson, an itinerant minstrel (partial).

Here in a lonely spot the bones repose,
Of one who murdered rhyme and slaughtered prose;
Sense he defied and grammar set at nought
Yet some have read his books and even bought
For want of art his virtues made amends.

Recorded in Snodland, Kent, on Thomas and Mary Palmer (d. 1407).

Palmers al our faders were
I, a Palmer, livyd here
And travylled till worne wythe age
I endyd this worlds pylgramage
On the blyst Assention day
In the cherful month of May
A thowsand wyth fowre hundryd seven
And took my jorney hense to Heuen

All Saints, Kirtlington, Cambridgeshire.

Here restith the Cors of Edward Myrfin Gentilman. Borne in
the Citie of London, educated in good Vertu and Lernying,
travelled through all the Countries and notable Cities, Princes
Courts, with other famous Places of Europe and likewise of
the Isles of Greece and soe to the Turks Courte, then being
in the Citie of Aleppo on the Borders between Armenia and
Siria, and so returning through Jury to Jerusalem, and soe
to Damasco from thence passing by diverse Countries with
sondrie Adventure arrived at length in his own native Citie,
where shortly after he ended his life, in the year of Our Lord
MCCCCC fifty and three, and in the XXVII yere of his age.

Roxburgh, Roxburghshire, Scotland. Andrew Gemmels was the inspiration for Edie Ochiltree in Sir Walter Scott's novel, *The Antiquary*.

BEHOLD THE END O' IT

THE BODY OF THE GENTLEMAN BEGGAR
ANDREW GEMMELS
ALIAS EDIE OCHILTREE
WAS INTERRED HERE
WHO DIED AT
ROXBURGH NEWTOWN
IN 1793 AGED 106.

ERECTED
BY W THOMSON FARMER
OVER-ROXBURGH
1849.

Abney Park Cemetery, Stoke Newington, London.

WILLIAM BOOTH
FOUNDER & 1ST GENERAL OF
THE SALVATION ARMY
BORN 1829
BORN AGAIN OF THE SPIRIT 1845
FOUNDED THE SALVATION ARMY 1865
WENT TO HEAVEN 20TH AUGUST 1912

ALSO

CATHERINE BOOTH
THE MOTHER OF THE SALVATION ARMY
BORN 1829
WENT TO HEAVEN 4TH OCTOBER 1890

Bath Abbey, Somerset.

IN MEMORY OF
SIR ISAAC PITMAN K-
1813 – 1897

INVENTOR OF PITMAN'S SHORTHAND
His aims were steadfast, his mind
Original, his work prodigious, the achievement
World-wide. His life was ordered in
Service to God and duty to man.

St Peter, Wolvercote, Oxfordshire, on William Meredith, organist of New College, Oxford.

Here lies one blown out of breath,
Who lived a merry life, and died a Merideth.

SS Peter and Paul, Stondon Massey, Essex.

A FATHER OF MUSICK
TO THE GLORY OF GOD AND IN MEMORY OF
WILLIAM BYRD
WHO LIVED AT STONDON PLACE
IN THIS PARISH FOR THE LAST THIRTY YEARS OF HIS LIFE.
HE DIED 4 JULY 1623 AGED EIGHTY.
THIS TABLET WAS ERECTED IN 1923 IN CELE
BRATION OF THE TERCENTENARY OF HIS DEATH.

St Sepulchre without Newgate, Holborn, London.

THIS WINDOW
IS DEDICATED TO THE MEMORY OF
SIR HENRY WOOD C.H.
FOUNDER AND FOR MANY YEARS CONDUCTOR
OF THE PROMENADE CONCERTS 1895–1944
HE OPENED THE DOOR TO A NEW WORLD OF
SENSE AND FEELING TO MILLIONS OF HIS FELLOWS
HE GAVE HIS LIFE FOR MUSIC
AND BROUGHT MUSIC TO THE PEOPLE
HIS ASHES REST BENEATH

St Andrew, Hampstead, Essex.

THE REMAINS OF WILLIAM HARVEY
DISCOVERER OF THE CIRCULATION OF THE BLOOD,
WERE REVERENTIALLY PLACED IN THIS SARCOPHAGUS, BY
THE ROYAL COLLEGE OF PHYSICIANS OF LONDON
IN THE YEAR 1883

Old Hill Burying Ground, Newburyport, Massachusetts.

Here lie ye Remains of NATHAN HALE Esq.
who died May 9, 1767. Aged 76 Years
He was a Physician of much Experience & Considerable
Eminence & highly esteemed in his Profession which he
carefully attended, distributing his Services without
Distinction to Rich & Poor. He was for many Years
a justice of the Peace which office he faithfully executed
with integrity & without Partiality. He was a Gentleman

**St Paul's Cathedral, London. A microscope is etched between the dates.
The quotation is from Hooke's description of the 'small silver-colour'd
book-worm' from his *Micrographia*, and is engraved around the
perimeter of the memorial.**

ROBERT HOOKE
1635 1703

One
of the most
ingenious men who
ever lived

Fellow of
The Royal Society
Prof of Geometry
Gresham College

Surveyor to
The City of London
Friend & colleague
Of Sir Christopher
Wren

It appears to the naked eye, a small glistering Pearl-colour'd Moth, which upon the removing of Books and Papers in the Summer, is often observ'd very nimbly to scud, and pack away to some lurking cranney, where it may the better protect it self from any appearing dangers.

St Nicholas of Myra, Worth Matravers, Dorset. William Jenner is generally credited with the first cowpox inoculation, though Bejamin Jesty's experiments predate Jenner's.

To the Memory
of
Benj. Jesty (of Downshay)
Who departed this Life,
April 16th 1816
Aged 79 Years.
He was born at Yetminster in this
County and was an upright honest
Man: particularly noted for having
been the first Person (known) that
Introduced the Cow Pox
by Inoculation, and who from
his great strength of mind made the
Experiment from the (Cow) on
his Wife and two Sons in the Year 1744.

All Saints, Shirburn, on Thomas Phelps, a self-taught astronomer, having risen from stable hand in the household of Thomas Parker, 1st Earl of Macclesfield (1666–1732), to higher positions, and was given charge of the observatory by George Parker, 2nd Earl of Macclesfield.

Near this Place are Deposited
The Remains
Of
Mr. Thomas Phelps,
Who without the Aids of Education
Acquired by his own Industry
A competent Skill
In Mathematical as well as other Branches
of Knowledge,
and had for many Years
the Management of the Observatory
belonging to
the Earl of Macclesfield

Learn Reader from His Example
that Length of Days are the Reward
of Temperance and Frugality
and that an honest, diligent and benevolent Man
is both an honour and a Blessing
to the World he lives in.

He died much lamented in the 84 Year of his age
and
His Patron in testimony of his services
inscribed
This Stone to his Memory

All Saints Church, Spofforth, North Yorkshire, on John Metcalfe. Despite his blindness from smallpox at the age of four, he was married and had numerous careers, including musician, horse trader, fish supplier, textile merchant and stage-wagon operator. He became a great road builder, laying nearly 200 miles of roads in Yorkshire, Lancashire, Derbyshire, and Cheshire.

Here lies John Metcalfe, one whose infant sight
Felt the dark pressure of an endless night;
Yet such the fervour of his dauntless mind
His limbs full strung, his spirit unconfin'd,
That, long ere yet life's bolder years began,
His sightless efforts mark'd the aspiring man;
Nor mark'd in vain High deeds his manhood dar'd
And commerce, travel, both his ardour shar'd.

'Twas his a guide's unerring aid to lend;
O'er trackless wastes to bid new roads extend;
And when Rebellion rear'd her giant size,
'Twas his to burn with patriotic enterprise,
For parting wife and babes one pang to feel,
Then welcome danger of his country's weal.

Reader! Like him, exert thy utmost talent giv'n.
Reader! Like him, adore the bounteous hand of Heav'n.

He died on the 26th of April 1810
In the 93d year of his age.

St John the Baptist, Bromsgrove, Worcestershire.

SACRED
TO THE MEMORY OF THOMAS SCAIFE,
late engineer on the Birmingham and Gloucester Railway,
who lost his life at Bromsgrove Station by explosion of
an engine boiler. Tuesday the 10th of Nov. 1840.

He was 28 yrs of age, highly esteemed by his fellow workmen
for his many amiable qualities, and his Death will be long lamented
by all those who had the pleasure of his acquaintance.
The following lines were composed by an unknown friend
as a Memento of the worthiness of the Deceased.

> My engine now is cold and still,
> No water does my boiler fill.
> My coke affords its flames no more,
> My days of usefulness are o'er.
> My wheels deny their noted speed,
> No more my guiding hands they need.
> My whistle too has lost its tone,
> Its shrill and thrilling sound has gone.
> My valves are now thrown open wide,
> My flanges all refuse to guide.
> My clacks, although once so strong,
> Refuse to aid the busy throng.
> No more I feel each urging breath,
> My steam is now condens'd in death.
> Life's railway's o'er each station's pass,
> In death I'm stopp'd & rest at last.
> Farewell dear friends and cease to weep,
> In Christ I'm safe in him I sleep.'

THIS STONE WAS ERECTED AT THE JOINT EXPENSE
OF HIS FELLOW WORKMEN 1842.

**Kensal Green Cemetery, London, on the father of Isambard Kingdom Brunel
(who is buried in the same family grave).**

SIR MARC ISAMBARD BRUNEL

CIVIL ENGINEER

BORN AT RACQUEVILLE IN NORMANDY APRIL 25 1769 DIED IN LONDON
DECEMBER 18 1840

HE HAS RAISED HIS OWN MONUMENT BY HIS PUBLIC WORKS
AT PORTSMOUTH CHATHAM AND THE THAMES TUNNEL

St Pieterskerk, Leiden, The Netherlands, on Ludolph van Ceulen (1540–1610), who computed pi to 35 digits. His original memorial on which, quite remarkably, the discovery was first published, was lost in the early nineteenth century. A new one was erected in 2005 reproducing the original inscription, the text and shape of which (a circle) was preserved in a contemporary local guidebook. It contains his upper and lower bounds for pi (tr. from Dutch, partial).

WHEN THE DIAMETER IS

10000000000000000000000000000000000000

THE CIRCUMFERENCE IS GREATER THAN

3.14159265358979323846264338327950288
10000000000000000000000000000000000000

AND LESS THAN

3.14159265358979323846264338327950289
10000000000000000000000000000000000000

Alter Friedhof, Freiburg, Germany, on Thaddäus Rinderle, mathematician (tr. from German).

RINDERLE
PROFESSOR
BORN ON FEBRUARY 3RD, 1748
DIED ON OCTOBER 7TH, 1824

HE DETERMINED MANY THINGS, MATHEMATICALLY
WITH DIGITS AND LETTERS.
BUT THE HOUR OF DEATH REMAINS
MORE UNKNOWN THAN X

Westminster Abbey, London, on Paul Dirac, with a simplified version of his equation for the electron.

1902

P.A.M.

DIRAC O.M.

PHYSICIST

$$i\gamma \times \gamma\psi = m\psi$$

1984

St Mary, Rougham, Norwich. The headstone shows a Vickers Vimy bi-plane. Four months after North died, the plane he designed travelled from Newfoundland to Ireland, making the first non-stop crossing of the Atlantic Ocean.

Here lies all that was good of
THOMAS KEPPEL NORTH OBE
Youngest son of the late Keppel North
of this parish who died at Crayforth in
the county of Kent on the 19th day of February
in the year of our Lord 1919 aged 43 years.
He was the superintendent of Vickers
Works and designed the first aeroplane
to cross the Atlantic Ocean.

St Andrew, Melton, Suffolk.

IN MEMORY OF

SEARLES V. WOOD JUNR.

OF MARTLESHAM

WHO DIED 14TH DECR. 1884 AGED 54 YEARS

HE WAS THE FIRST GEOLOGIST TO UNDERTAKE

THE DETAILED MAPPING OVER AN EXTENSIVE AREA

OF THE VARIOUS SUB-DIVISIONS OF THE GLACIAL DRIFT

A TASK OF INFINITE LABOUR AND OF

GREAT PRACTICAL AND SCIENTIFIC IMPORTANCE.

St Michael, Gittisham, Devon, on Henry Ince, who devised the plan to tunnel beneath the great rock during the Great Siege of Gibraltar (June 1779–February 1783) resulting in a labyrinth of tunnels where British canons were mounted overlooking the isthmus linking the peninsula to Spain.

In Memory of
Lieut HENRY INCE,
late of the Royal Garrison Battn,
Gibraltar, the works of which For
tress bear lasting testimony to
his skill industry and zeal.
After serving his Majesty 49
Years he retired full of honor to
this place and closing in piety, the
remains of a useful life, died
October 9th, 1808
Aged 72.
His principal service was in the Soldier
Artificer Company, the first unit of the
Corps of Royal Engineers.

St Mary the Virgin, Studland, Dorset.

TO THE HONOURED MEMORY

OF

SERJEANT WILLIAM LAWRENCE

OF THE 40TH REGIMENT OF FOOT

WHO AFTER A LONG AND EVENTFUL LIFE

IN THE SERVICE OF HIS COUNTRY

PEACEFULLY ENDED HIS DAYS AT STUDLAND,

NOVEMBER 11TH, 1869.

HE SERVED WITH HIS DISTINGUISHED REGIMENT

IN THE WAR IN SOUTH AMERICA 1805

AND THROUGH THE WHOLE OF THE PENINSULAR WAR 1808–1813

HE RECEIVED A SILVER MEDAL AND NO LESS THAN TEN CLASPS
FOR THE BATTLES IN WHICH HE WAS ENGAGED

ROLEIA   VIMIERA   TALAVERA

CIUDAD   RODRIGO

BADAJOZ

(IN WHICH DESPERATE ASSAULT BEING ONE OF THE VOULUNTEERS FOR THE
FORLORN HOPE HE WAS MOST SEVERELY WOUNDED)

VITTORIA PYRENNES NIVELLES

ORTHES TOULOUSE

HE ALSO FOUGHT IN THE GLORIOUS VICTORY OF

WATERLOO

JUNE 18TH, 1815

While serving with his regiment during the
Occupation of Paris by the Allied Armies
Serjeant Lawrence married Clotilde Clairet
at St. Germain-en-Laye who died September 26 1853
and was buried beneath this Spot

Saint Vedast-alias-Foster, London.

In memory of

PETRO

MAJOR

WLADIMIR VASSILIEVITCH

PETROPAVLOVSKY

1888–1971

SOLDIER OF THE TSAR,

OF FRANCE, OF ENGLAND

This tablet was erected by
George Courtauld and
Other friends

'This was a Man'

St Leonard, Hythe, Kent, on Lionel Lukin (1742–1834).

THIS LIONEL LUKIN

WAS THE FIRST WHO BUILT

A LIFE BOAT AND WAS THE ORIGINAL INVENTOR OF THAT

PRINCIPLE OF SAFETY

BY WHICH MANY LIVES AND MUCH PROPERTY

HAS BEEN PRESERVED FROM SHIPWRECK

AND HE OBTAINED FOR IT THE KINGS PATENT

IN THE YEAR 1785.

St Lawrence, Ramsgate, Kent (1903).

This marks the wreck of Robert Woolward who sailed the seas for fifty-five years. When Resurrection gun fires, the wreck will be raised by the Angelic Salvage Co. surveyed and if found worthy, refitted and started on the voyage to Eternity.

Richmond Cemetery, Grove Road, Richmond (b. 1812), Surrey, on Tom Richardson, cricketer and fast bowler, who played for Surrey and England. He took 290 wickets in one season, a record that stood for 33 years. His headstone depicts stumps and a cricket ball.

IN LOVEING MEMORY

OF

TOM RICHARDSON

SURREY AND ENGLAND CRICKETER

HE BOWLED HIS BEST

BUT WAS HIMSELF BOWLED

BY THE BEST

ON JUL 2ND 1912

St Lawrence, Eyam, Derbyshire, on Harry Bagshaw who played first-class cricket for Derbyshire between 1887 and 1902 and was also a cricket umpire. His headstone depicts stumps, wickets, a ball, and a bat.

TO

THE DEAR MEMORY OF

HARRY BAGSHAW

WHO DIED JANY 31ST 1927

AGED 67 YEARS.

FROM 1888 TO 1924 WITH

DERBYSHIRE & M.C.C.

WELL PLAYED.

FOR WHEN THE ONE GREAT SCORER COMES

TO WRITE AGAINS'T YOUR NAME

HE WRITES — NOT THAT YOU WON OR LOST

BUT HOW YOU PLAYED THE GAME.

Chapter 3

Let Us Now Praise Famous Men – And Women

St Alban's Cathedral, Hertfordshire.

Here lieth interred the body of
Saint Alban,
A citizen of Old Verulam,
Of whom this town took denomination,
And from the ruins of which City,
this town did arise.
He was the first Martyr of England,
And suffered his martyrdom on the 17th day of June
In the year of Man's Redemption, 293.

St Augustine's Abbey, Canterbury, Kent.

St Augustine
Site of grave
1st Archbishop of Canterbury
597–605
d. 605

Westminster Abbey, London.

IN THE 900TH YEAR OF THE ROYAL
FOUNDATION OF THE MONASTERY
The Dean and Chapter
of the Collegiate Church of St Peter in
Westminster placed this memorial to
CAEDMON
who first among the English made verses

Battle Abbey, Hastings, Kent.

THE TRADITIONAL SITE OF
THE HIGH ALTAR OF BATTLE ABBEY
FOUNDED TO COMMEMORATE

THE VICTORY OF DUKE WILLIAM
ON 14 OCTOBER 1066
THE HIGH ALTAR WAS PLACED TO MARK
THE SPOT WHERE KING HAROLD DIED.

Priory Gardens, Coventry (partial).

GODIVA, Lady of Coventry
(died 10th September 1067) and her husband
LEOFRIC, Earl of Mercia
(died 28th September 1057) were buried here in the church of
Benedictine monastery they founded in 1043 on the site of St Osburg's
nunnery,
sacked by the Danes in 1016.

St Michael, Paternoster Royal, London.

Richard Whittington
Four times
Mayor of London
Founded and was buried
In this church
1422

St Michael and All Angels, Hathersage, Derbyshire.

HERE LIES BURIED
LITTLE JOHN
THE FRIEND & LIEUTENANT OF
ROBIN HOOD
IN A COTTAGE (NOW DESTROYED)
TO THE EAST OF THE CHURCHYARD
THE GRAVE IS MARKED BY
THIS OLD HEADSTONE & FOOTSTONE
AND IS UNDERNEATH THIS OLD YEW TREE.

Westminster Abbey, London, on Margaret Beaufort, Countess of Richmond and Derby, composed by Erasmus (tr. from Latin).

Margaret of Richmond, mother of Henry VII, grandmother of Henry VIII who gave a salary to three monks of this convent and founded a grammar school at Wimborne, and to a preacher throughout England, and to two interpreters of Scripture, one at Oxford, the other at Cambridge, where she likewise founded two colleges, one to Christ, and the other to St John, his disciple. Died A.D.1509, III Kalends of July [29 June].

Basilica di Santa Maria del Fiore, Florence, Italy, on Sir John Hawkwood (c. 1320–94), an English mercenary active in Italy (where he was known as Giovanni Acuto), from a fresco by Paolo Uccello (tr. from Latin).

John Hawkwood, British knight, most prudent leader of his age and most expert in the art of war.

St Magnus the Martyr, London (partial).

TO THE

MEMORY OF

MILES COVERDALE

WHO CONVINCED THAT THE PURE

WORD OF GOD

OUGHT TO BE THE SOLE RULE

OF OUR FAITH

AND GUIDE OF OUR PRACTICE

LABOURED EARNESTLY FOR

ITS DIFFUSION

AND WITH A VIEW OF AFFORDING

THE MEANING OF READING AND

HEARING IN THEIR OWN TONGUE

THE WONDERFUL WORKS OF GOD

NOT ONLY TO HIS

OWN COUNTRYMEN BUT TO

THE NATIONS THAT SIT IN DARKNESS

AND TO EVERY CHURCH

WHERESOEVER THE ENGLISH
LANGUAGE MIGHT BE SPOKEN
HE SPENT MANY YEARS OF HIS LIFE
PREPARING A TRANSLATION
OF THE SCRIPTURES.
ON THE IV OF OCTOBER MDXXXV
THE FIRST COMPLETE
ENGLISH PRINTED VERSION OF
THE BIBLE
WAS PUBLISHED UNDER
HIS DIRECTION.

St Dunstan, Canterbury, Kent.

BENEATH THIS FLOOR
IS THE VAULT OF THE
ROPER FAMILY IN WHICH
IS INTERRED THE HEAD OF
SIR THOMAS MORE
OF ILLUSTRIOUS MEMORY
SOMETIME LORD CHANCELLOR
OF ENGLAND WHO WAS
BEHEADED ON TOWER HILL
6TH JULY 1535

ECCLESIA ANGLICANA LIBERA SIT
[MAY THE ENGLISH CHURCH BE FREE]

St George's Chapel, Windsor, Berkshire.

IN A VAULT
BENEATH THIS MARBLE SLAB
ARE DEPOSTED THE REMAINS
OF
JANE SEYMOUR QUEEN OF KING HENRY VIII
1537

KING HENRY VIII
1547

CHARLES I
1648

AND

AN INFANT CHILD OF QUEEN ANNE

Leicester Cathedral, Leicestershire. The bones of Richard III were discovered beneath a car park on the site previously occupied by Greyfriars Priory Church in Leicester. He was reburied in the Cathedral in March 2015 under his motto, which is translated 'loyalty binds me'.

RICHARD III
1452–1485
Loyaulte me lie

Westminster Abbey, London, on Elizabeth I (tr. From Latin, partial).

Sacred to memory: Religion to its primitive purity restored, peace settled, money restored to its just value, domestic rebellion quelled, France relieved when involved with intestine divisions; the Netherlands supported; the Spanish Armada vanquished; Ireland almost lost by rebels, eased by routing the Spaniard; the revenues of both universities much enlarged by a Law of Provisions; and lastly, all England enriched. Elizabeth, a most prudent governor 45 years, a victorious and triumphant Queen, most strictly religious, most happy, by a calm and resigned death at her 70th year left her mortal remains, till by Christ's Word they shall rise to immortality, to be deposited in the Church [the Abbey], by her established and lastly founded. She died the 24th of March, 1602 [1603], of her reign the 45th year, of her age the 70th.

Broad Street, Oxford, Oxfordshire.

Opposite this point
near the Cross in the
middle of Broad Street
HUGH LATIMER
one time Bishop of Worcester,
NICHOLAS RIDLEY
Bishop of London, and
THOMAS CRANMER
Archbishop of Canterbury,
were burnt for their
faith in 1555 and 1556.

St Giles, Cripplegate, London.

SIR MARTIN FROBISHER KT

OF

NORMANTON, YORKSHIRE

1535 − 1594

INTERRED IN THIS CHURCH

SEEKER OF THE NORTH WEST PASSAGE

1576–7–8

FAMED FOR HIS DECISIVE ACTION AGAINST

THE SPANISH ARMADA

St Mary the Virgin, Mortlake, London.

Near this place lie the remains of
JOHN DEE MA
Clerk in holy orders
1527 − 1609
Astronomer, Geographer
Mathematician
Adviser to Queen Elizabeth I

Sidney Sussex College, Cambridge.

Near to
This place was buried
On 25 May 1960 the head of
OLIVER CROMWELL
Lord Protector of the Common-
wealth of England, Scotland &
Ireland, Fellow Commoner
of this College 1616.

St Margaret, Westminster.

WITHIN THE CHANCEL OF THIS CHURCH WAS INTERRED
THE BODY OF THE GREAT SIR WALTER RALEIGH KT
ON THE DAY HE WAS BEHEADED
IN OLD PALACE YARD, WESTMINSTER
OCT 29TH ANNO DOM. 1618

READER – Should you reflect on his errors
Remember his many virtues
And that he was mortal.

St Paul's Cathedral, London, formerly on a tablet hung from a pillar, on Sir Philip Sidney.

England, Netherlands, the Heavens, and the Arts
The Souldiers, and the World, have made Six Parts.
Of Nobility, SYDNEY! for none will suppose
that a small Heap of Stones can SYDNEY inclose
His Body hath England, for she it bred,
Netherlands his Bloud, in her Defence shed;
The Heavens have his Soule, the Arts have his Fame
All Souldiers the Grief, the World his good Name.

Westminster Abbey, London.

O RARE BEN JONSON

St Nicholas, Deptford Green, London.

NEAR THIS SPOT LIE THE MORTAL REMAINS OF
CHRISTOPHER MARLOWE
WHO MET HIS UNTIMELY DEATH
IN DEPTFORD ON MAY 30TH 1593

Cut is the branch that might have grown full straight
Dr Faustus

Holy Trinity, Stratford-upon-Avon, on William Shakespeare.

GOOD FREND FOR IESUS SAKE FORBEARE,
TO DIG THE DUST ENCLOASED HEARE:
BLESTE BE YE MAN THAT SPARES THES STONES,
AND CURST BE HE THAT MOVES MY BONES.

St Paul's Cathedral, London. Said to have been inscribed on a wall above John Donne's grave the day after his funeral.

Reader, I am to let thee know,
Donne's body only lies below;
For could the grave his soul comprise,
Earth would be richer than the skies.

Royal Observatory, Greenwich, London, removed from St Margaret, Lee, London (tr. from Latin).

Beneath this gravestone, Edmond Halley,
unquestionably the most eminent of the astronomers
of his age, rests peacefully with his dearest wife. So
that the reader may know what kind and how great

a man [he] was, read his various writings in which
he dignified, embellished and strengthened almost all
the arts and sciences.
And therefore, as he was a man so greatly cherished
by his fellow-citizens during his lifetime, so let a grateful
posterity venerate his memory. Born in the year of our
Lord 1656. Died 1741/2. This stone was consecrated
to excellent parents by two devoted daughters in the
year 1742.

St Paul's Cathedral, London (tr. from Latin).

HERE IN ITS FOUNDATIONS
LIES THE ARCHITECT OF THIS CHURCH AND CITY,
CHRISTOPHER WREN,
WHO LIVED BEYOND NINETY YEARS,
NOT FOR HIS OWN PROFIT BUT FOR THE PUBLIC GOOD.
READER, IF YOU SEEK HIS MONUMENT
LOOK AROUND YOU.
DIED 25 FEB. 1723, AGE 91

Westminster Abbey, London (tr. from Latin).

HERE LIES THAT WHICH WAS MORTAL OF ISAAC NEWTON

All Saints, High Laver Church, Essex.

IN GRATEFUL MEMORY OF
JOHN LOCKE
1632–1704, WHO LIES BURIED HERE
HIS PHILOSOPHY GUIDED
THE FOUNDERS OF
THE UNITED STATES OF AMERICA
ERECTED BY THE AMERICAN AND
BRITISH COMMONWEALTH ASSOCIATION
OF THE UNITED STATES 1957.

United First Parish Church, Quincy, Massachusetts.

Beneath these Walls
Are deposited the Mortal Remains of
JOHN ADAMS,
Son of John and Susanna [Boylston] Adams,
Second President of the United States.
Born 19/30 October 1785.
On the fourth of July 1776
He pledged his Life, Fortune and Sacred Honour
To the INDEPENDENCE OF HIS COUNTRY.
On the third of September 1783
He affixed his Seal to the definitive Treaty with Great Britain
Which acknowledged that Independence,
And consummated the Redemption of his Pledge.
On the fourth of July 1826
He was summoned
To the Independence of Immortality,
And to the JUDGMENT OF HIS GOD.
This House will bear witness to his Piety:
This Town, his Birth-Place, to his Munificence:
History to his Patriotism:
Posterity to the Depth and Compass of his Mind.

Monticello, Charlottesville, Virginia. Thomas Jefferson left highly detailed instructions for his tomb, prescribing that '... on the faces of the Obelisk the following inscription, & not a word more' be engraved. It contains no reference to his tenure of the office of President of the United States – twice. He and John Adams died within hours of one another, on 4 July.

"HERE WAS BURIED
THOMAS JEFFERSON
AUTHOR OF THE
DECLARATION
OF
AMERICAN INDEPENDENCE

OF THE
STATUTE OF VIRGINIA
FOR
RELIGIOUS FREEDOM
AND FATHER OF THE
UNIVERSITY OF VIRGINA

BORN APRIL 2 1743 O.S.
DIED JULY 4 1826"

West Point, New York.

IN MEMORY OF
MARGARET CORBIN
A HEROINE OF THE REVOLUTION
KNOWN AS CAPTAIN MOLLY
1751 – 1800
WHO AT THE BATTLE OF FORT WASHINGTON, NEW YORK CITY, WHEN HER
HUSBAND JOHN CORBIN WAS KILLED, KEPT HIS FIELD PIECE IN ACTION
UNTIL SEVERELY WOUNDED AND THEREAFTER, BY AN ACT OF CONGRESS,
RECEIVED HALF THE PAY AND ALLOWANCES OF
"A SOLDIER IN THE SERVICE"
SHE LIVED, DIED AND WAS BURIED ON THE HUDSON RIVER BANK, NEAR TH
VILLAGE CALLED HIGHLAND FALLS. IN APPRECIATION OF HER DEEDS FOR
THE CAUSE OF LIBERTY, AND THAT HER HEROISM MAY NOT BE FORGOTTEN,
HER DUST WAS REMOVED TO THIS SPOT AND THIS MEMORIAL ERECTED BY
THE NATIONAL SOCIETY OF THE DAUGHTERS OF THE AMERICAN REVOLUTIO
IN NEW YORK STATE
1926

Westminster Abbey, on Aphra Behn (1640–89), playwright, poet, translator, and fiction writer.

Here lies a Proof that Wit can never be
Defence enough against Mortality.

St Nicholas, Cheswick, London on William Hogarth (1697–1764), by David Garrick.

Farewell, great Painter of Mankind
Who reach'd the noblest point of Art,
Whose pictur'd Morals charm the mind.
And through the eye correct the Heart.
If Genius fire thee, reader stay,
If Nature move thee, drop a tear:
If neither touch thee, turn away,
For Hogarth's honour'd Dust lies here.

Westminster Abbey, London.

Here lyes
HENRY PURCELL, Esqr.
Who left this life
And is gone to that Blessed Place
Where only his Harmony
can be exceeded.
Obijt 21 die Novembrs
Anno Aetatis suae 37mo
Anno Domini 1695

Chichester Cathedral, memorial set into the floor, showing two planets. The quotation is from Holst's *Hymn of Jesus*.

GUSTAV HOLST
1874–1934
THE HEAVENLY SPHERES MAKE MUSIC FOR US

Winchester Cathedral, Hampshire.

In Memory of
JANE AUSTEN
Youngest daughter of the late
Revd GEORGE AUSTEN,

Formerly Rector of Steventon in this County,
She departed this Life on the 18th of July, 1817,
Aged 41, after a long illness supported with
The patience and the hopes of a Christian.

The benevolence of her heart,
The sweetness of her tempter, and
The extraordinary endowments of her mind
Obtained the regard of all who knew her, and
The warmest love of her intimate connections.

Their grief is in proportion to their affection
They know their loss to be irreparable,
But in their deepest affliction they are consoled
By a firm though humble hope that her charity,
Devotion, faith and purity, rendered
Her soul and acceptable in the sight of her
REDEEMER.

Highgate Cemetery, London.

OF THOSE IMMORTAL DEAD WHO LIVE AGAIN

IN MINDS MADE BETTER BY THEIR PRESENCE

HERE LIES THE BODY

OF

'GEORGE ELIOT'

MARY ANN CROSS

BORN 22 NOVEMBER 1819

DIED 22 DECEMBER 1880

St Mary Magdalen, Hucknall Torkard, Nottinghamshire, on George Gordon, 6th Baron Byron (1788–1824).

… He died at Missolonghi, in Western Greece, on the
19th April 1824,
Engaged in the glorious attempt to

Restore that country to her ancient
Freedom and renown.
His sister, the Honourable
Augusta Maria Leigh,
Placed this tablet to his memory.

English Cemetery, Rome.

PERCY BYSSHE SHELLEY

COR CORDIUM*

NATUS IV AUG. MDCCXCII

OBIIT VII JUL. MDCCCXXII

NOTHING OF HIM THAT DOTH FADE

BUT DOTH SUFFER A SEA-CHANGE

INTO SOMETHING RICH AND STRANGE.

Heart of hearts. The quotation is from Shakespeare's *The Tempest* (I.ii.402).

St Peter, Bournemouth, Dorset.

IN THIS

CHURCHYARD LIE

THE MORTAL REMAINS OF

MARY SHELLEY

AUTHOR OF "FRANKENSTEIN"

HER FATHER WILLIAM

AUTHOR OF "POLITICAL JUSTICE"

HER MOTHER MARY

AUTHOR OF "THE RIGHTS OF WOMEN"

HER SON PERCY, JANE HIS WIFE

AND THE HEART OF

PERCY BYSSHE

HER HUSBAND

THE POET

English Cemetery, Rome, on John Keats (1795–1821).

This Grave
Contains all that was Mortal
of a
YOUNG ENGLISH POET
Who
on his Death Bed,
In the Bitterness of his Heart
at the Malicious Power of his Enemies,
Desired
these Words to be engraved on his Tomb Stone.

Here lies One
Whose Name was writ in Water.

Feb 24th 1821

St Mary, Scarborough, North Yorkshire.

Anne Brontë
1820–1849
novelist and poet

The original headstone reads

Here lie the remains of Anne Brontë
Daughter of the Revd P Brontë
Incumbent of Haworth Yorkshire
She died Aged 28 May 28th 1849

The text contains one error
Anne Brontë was aged 29 when she died

This plaque was paced here in 2011
by the Brontë Soceity

St Botolph, Helpston, Cambridgeshire.

SACRED TO THE MEMORY OF
JOHN CLARE
THE NORTHAMPTONSHIRE PEASANT POET
BORN JULY 13 1793 DIED MAY 20 1864

HERE Rest the HOPES
And Ashes of
JOHN CLARE

A POET IS BORN NOT MADE

**Victoria Embankment Gardens, London,
on the statue of Robert Burns (1759–96).**

The poetic genius of my country found me at the plough and threw her
inspiring mantle over me. She bade me sing the loves, the joys, the rural
scenes and rural pleasures of my native soil, in my native tongue. I tuned
my wild, artless notes as she inspired.

West Cemetery, Amherst, Massachusetts.

EMILY DICKINSON
BORN DEC. 10 1830

CALLED BACK
MAY 15, 1886

Old Bennington Cemetery, Bennington, Vermont.

ROBERT LEE FROST
MAR 26, 1874 – JAN 29, 1963
I HAD A LOVER'S QUARREL WITH THE WORLD

St Michael, Stinsford, Dorset.

HERE LIES THE HEART OF
THOMAS HARDY OM
SON OF THOMAS AND JEMIMA HARDY
HE WAS BORN AT UPPER BOCKHAMPTON 2 JUNE 1840
AND DIED AT MAXGATE DORCHESTER 11 JANUARY 1928
HIS ASHES REST IN POET'S CORNER WESTMINSTER ABBEY

**Père Lachaise Cemetery, Paris, on Oscar Wilde (1854–1900),
from *The Ballad of Reading Gaol* (partial).**

And alien tears will fill for him
Pity's long broken urn,
For his mourners will be outcast men,
And outcasts always mourn.

Bunhill Fields, London.

THIS MEMORIAL IS THE RESULT OF AN APPEAL
IN THE CHRISTIAN WORLD NEWSPAPER
TO THE BOYS AND GIRLS OF ENGLAND FOR FUNDS
TO PLACE A SUITABLE MEMORIAL UPON THE GRAVE
OF
DANIEL DE-FOE
IT REPRESENTS THE UNITED CONTRIBUTIONS
OF SEVENTEEN HUNDRED PERSONS
SEPTR. 1870

Drumcliff, County Sligo, Ireland.

Cast a cold Eye
On Life, on Death.
Horseman, pass by!
W.B. YEATS

June 13th 1865
January 28th 1939

St Lawrence, Ludlow, Shropshire. The quotation is from Housman's poem 'Parta Quies'.

IN MEMORY OF

ALFRED EDWARD HOUSMAN

M.A. OXON.

KENNEDY PROFESSOR OF LATIN

AND FELLOW OF TRINITY COLLEGE

IN THE UNIVERSITY OF CAMBRIDGE

AUTHOR OF

A SHROPSHIRE LAD

BORN 26 MARCH 1859

DIED 30 APRIL 1936

GOODNIGHT, ENSURED RELEASE

IMPERISHABLE PEACE:

HAVE THESE FOR YOURS

St Cross, Oxford, Oxfordshire, on Kenneth Grahame (1859–1932), author of *The Wind in the Willows*.

TO

THE BEAUTIFUL MEMORY

OF KENNETH GRAHAME

HUSBAND OF ELSPETH

AND

FATHER OF ALASTAIR

WHO PASSED THE RIVER

ON THE 6TH OF JULY 1932

LEAVING

CHILDHOOD & LITERATURE

THE MORE BLEST

FOR ALL TIME.

AND OF HIS SON

ALASTAIR GRAHAME

COMMONER OF CHRIST CHURCH

1920

All Saints, Minstead, Hampshire.

Steel True
Blade Straight
Arthur Conan Doyle
Knight
Patriot, Physician & Man of Letters.
22 May 1858 – 7 July 1930
And his beloved, his wife
Jean Conan Doyle
Reunited 27 June 1940

Monk's House, Rodmell, Lewes, East Sussex.
The quotation is from Woolf's novel, *The Waves*.

BENEATH THIS TREE ARE
BURIED THE ASHES OF
VIRGINIA WOOLF
Born January 25 1882,
Died March 28 1941.

Death is the enemy. Against you
I will fling myself, unvanquished
and unyielding o Death!
The waves broke on the shore.

St James the Great, Old Milverton, Warwickshire.

VERA MARY BRITTAIN
29 DECEMBER 1893
EASTER SUNDAY 29 MARCH 1970
AUTHOR OF TESTAMENT OF YOUTH
"BLESSED ARE THE PEACEMAKERS
FOR THEY SHALL BE
CALLED THE CHILDREN OF GOD"
MATTHEW V

St Michael, East Coker, Somerset.

"in my beginning is my end"

OF YOUR CHARITY
PRAY FOR THE REPOSE
OF THE SOUL OF
THOMAS STEARNS ELIOT
POET
26TH SEPTEMBER 1888 – 4TH JANUARY 1965

"in my end is my beginning"

St Thomas the Apostle, Heptonstall, West Yorkshire.

IN MEMORY
SYLVIA PLATH HUGHES
1932–1963

EVEN AMIDST FIERCE FLAMES
THE GOLDEN LOTUS CAN BE PLANTED

Cimetière de Plainpalais, Geneva on Jorge Francisco Isidoro Luis Borges KBE
(1899–1986). The front of the stone depicts a group of warriors and reproduces
a line from the Old English poem *The Battle of Maldon*, uttered by Byrtnoth
to his young warriors ('Do not be afraid'). The reverse of the stone depicts
a Viking ship and bears a line from the Old Norse *Volsunga Saga*, spoken
by Sigurd to Brynhild ('He took the sword Gram and laid the naked metal
between them'), quoted by Borges at the beginning of his short story *Ulrica*.

JORGE LUIS BORGES
... AND NE FORHTEDON NÁ

1899
1986

Hann tekr sverthtt Gram ok leggr i methal their a bert

De Ulrica a Javier Otárola

Parton Parish Church, Dumfries and Galloway, Scotland.

JAMES CLERK MAXWELL FRS FRSE
OF GLENAIR
1831 1879
HIS SHORT LIFE WAS RICH IN DISTINGUISHED CONTRIBUTIONS TO
EVERY BRANCH OF PHYSICAL SCIENCE — HEAT, LIGHT, MECHANICS,
ABOVE ALL, BY UNIFYING THE THEORIES OF ELECTRICITY AND
AND MAGNETISM HE ESTABLISHED A SURE FOUNDATION FOR
MODERN PHYSICS, ELECTRICAL ENGINEERING AND ASTRONOMY
AND PREPARED THE WAY FOR RADIO COMMUNICATION AND TELEVISION.

Kirkby Mallory, Leicestershire. This is the second of the two-part memorial plaque on Ada Lovelace (1815–52), the first containing her sonnet, also inscribed on a stone arch in the churchyard, erected by Ada's mother.

MATHEMATICAL ADA

always a bright and inquisitive child, she spent her early years with her mother at Kirkby Mallory Hall, after her parents separated. At the age of 19 she married William, Lord King, later Earl of Lovelace.

Ada is best known for her work alongside Charles Babbage on his 'Analytical Engine' in the 1840s. she was one of the first to write programmes for and predict the impact of this device, which came to be regarded as the forerunner of the modern computer. The U.S. Departmen of Defence named the ADA computer language after her.

Ada died of cancer in 1852, the age of 36 she is buried beside her father at Hucknall Notts. Ada requested a memorial with her sonnet 'The Rainbow' engraved on it, and so this monument was raised to her memory by her mother Lady Byron.

Sackville Park, Manchester.

Alan Mathison Turing
1912–1954
Father of Computer Science
Mathematician, Logician
Wartime Codebreaker
Victim of Prejudice

Highgate Cemetery, London.

KARL MARX

WORKERS OF ALL LANDS
UNITE

THE PHILOSOPHERS HAVE ONLY
INTERPRETED THE WORLD IN
VARIOUS WAYS. THE POINT
HOWEVER IS TO CHANGE IT.

Holy Trinity, Crockham Hill, Kent.

OCTAVIA HILL
1838   1912

NOBLE IN AIM, WISE IN METHOD, UNSWERVING IN FAITH AND COURAGE
SHE DEVOTED HER LIFE TO RAISING THE BODILY CONDITIONS
AND RENEWING THE SPIRITUAL STRENGTH OF HER FELLOW CITIZENS.
SHE WAS A PIONEER IN THE MATTER OF HOUSING REFORM AND
A FOUNDER OF THE NATIONAL TRUST FOR SECURING PLACES
OF NATURAL BEAUTY AND HISTORIC INTEREST FOR THE PUBLIC.

Westminster Abbey, London, composed by Zachary Macaulay (partial).

TO THE MEMORY OF
WILLIAM WILBERFORCE

...

FOR NEARLY HALF A CENTURY A MEMBER OF THE HOUSE OF COMMONS,
AND, FOR SIX PARLIAMENTS DURING THAT PERIOD,
ONE OF THE TWO REPRESENTATIVES FOR YORKSHIRE. IN AN AGE AND
COUNTRY FERTILE IN GREAT AND GOOD MEN,
HE WAS AMONG THE FOREMOST OF THOSE WHO FIXED THE
CHARACTER OF THEIR TIMES ...

HIS NAME WILL EVER BE SPECIALLY IDENTIFIED
WITH THOSE EXERTIONS WHICH, BY THE BLESSING OF GOD, REMOVED
FROM ENGLAND THE GUILT OF THE AFRICAN SLAVE TRADE,
AND PREPARED THE WAY FOR THE ABOLITION OF SLAVERY
IN EVERY COLONY OF THE EMPIRE

IN THE PROSECUTION OF THESE OBJECTS
HE RELIED, NOT IN VAIN, ON GOD;
BUT IN THE PROGRESS HE WAS CALLED TO ENDURE
GREAT OBLOQUY AND GREAT OPPOSITION:
HE OUTLIVED, HOWEVER, ALL ENMITY;
AND, IN THE EVENING OF HIS DAYS,
WITHDREW FROM PUBLIC LIFE AND PUBLIC OBSERVATION
TO THE BOSOM OF HIS FAMILY.
YET HE DIED NOT UNNOTICED OR FORGOTTEN BY HIS COUNTRY:
THE PEERS AND COMMONS OF ENGLAND, WITH THE LORD CHANCELLOR AND
THE SPEAKER AT THEIR HEAD,
IN SOLEMN PROCESSION FROM THEIR RESPECTIVE HOUSES,
CARRIED HIM TO HIS FITTING PLACE
AMONG THE MIGHTY DEAD AROUND,
HERE TO REPOSE: TILL, THROUGH THE MERITS OF JESUS CHRIST,
HIS ONLY REDEEMER AND SAVIOUR,
(WHOM, IN HIS LIFE AND IN HIS WRITINGS HE HAD DESIRED TO GLORIFY,)
HE SHALL RISE IN THE RESURRECTION OF THE JUST.

St Margaret, East Wellow, Hampshire.
The remarkably modest memorial to Florence Nightingale.

F. N.

Born 12 May 1820
Died 13 August 1910

St Martin's Place, London. The quotation on this memorial is taken from
Cavell's words to the Reverend Stirling Gahan, the Anglican chaplain who
visited her the night before her execution. She is buried in Norwich Cathedral.

HUMANITY

EDITH CAVELL

BRUSSELS

DAWN

OCTOBER 12TH

1915

PATRIOTISM IS NOT ENOUGH

I MUST HAVE NO HATRED OR

BITTERNESS FOR ANYONE

Weifang, Shandong Province, China, on a memorial made of granite
from the Isle of Mull to Eric Liddell (1902–45), whose story is
celebrated in the film *Chariots of Fire*.

Eric Liddell was born in Tianjin
of Scottish parents in 1902. His
career reached its peak with his
gold medal victory in the 400
metres event at the 1924 Olympic
games. He returned to China to work
in Tianjin as a teacher. Liddell was
interned in a camp at the present site
of the Weifang second Middle School and
died in this camp shortly before the

Japanese were defeated in 1945. He
embodied fraternal virtues and his
whole life was spent encouraging young
people to make their best contributions
to the betterment of mankind.

But those who wait on the Lord shall renew their strength;
They shall mount up with wings like eagles,
They shall run and not be weary,
They shall walk and not faint.
[Isaiah 40:31]

Valhalla Cemetery, Burbank, Los Angeles.

AMELIA EARHART
BORN: JULY 24 1898
DIED: JULY 2 1937

FLEW ATLANTIC OCEAN SOLO
MAY 20–21, 1932

FIRST TO FLY PACIFIC OCEAN,
HONOLOULU TO CALIFORNIA, SOLO
JANUARY 11–12, 1935

MOST FAMOUS AND ONE OF THE MOST
BELOVED WOMEN FLIERS IN HISTORY
OF AMERICAN AVIATION

Palapala Ho'omau Church, Kipahulu, Maui, Hawaii.

CHARLES A. LINDBERGH
BORN MICHIGAN 1902   DIED MAUI 1974

"... if take the wings of the morning,
and dwell in the uttermost parts of the sea ..."

Putney Vale Cemetery, London. The quotations are from the Wishing Cup of Tutankhamen.

HOWARD CARTER

EGYPTOLOGIST

DISCOVERER OF THE TOMB OF

TUTANKHAMUN, 1922

BORN 9 MAY 1874

DIED, 2 MARCH 1939

"May your spirit live, may you spend
Millions of years, you who love Thebes,
Sitting with your face to the north wind,
Your eyes beholding happiness"

"O night, spread thy wings over me as the imperishable stars"

Beacon Hill (private plot), Highclere, Hampshire.

GEORGE EDWARD STANHOPE MOLYNEUX

5TH EARL OF CARNARVON

26TH JUNE 1866

5TH APRIL 1923

DISCOVERER OF THE TOMB OF

KING TUTANKHAMEN

NOVEMBER 1922

IN COLLABORATION WITH

HOWARD CARTER

St Nicholas, Moreton, Dorset.

TO THE DEAR MEMORY OF

T.E. LAWRENCE

FELLOW OF ALL SOULS COLLEGE

OXFORD

BORN 16 AUGUST 1888

DIED 19 MAY 1935

THE HOUR IS COMING & NOW IS
WHEN THE DEAD SHALL HEAR
THE VOICE OF THE SON OF GOD
AND THEY THAT HEAR
SHALL LIVE

Westminster Abbey, London. On the ashes of Hugh Caswall Tremenheere Dowding (1882–1970), 1st Baron Dowding, Air Officer Commanding-in-Chief of RAF Fighter Command at the time of the Battle of Britain (1940). He is credited with building up Fighter Command before the Second World War and with a successful strategy of defence during the Battle of Britain.

DOWDING

AIR CHIEF MARSHAL

1882–1970

HE LED THE FEW IN

THE

BATTLE OF BRITAIN

Llanystumdwy Gwynedd, Wales.

Bedd
David Lloyd George
Y maen garw, a maen ei goron, — yw bedd
Gŵr i'w bobl fu'n wron;
Dyfrliw hardd yw Dwyfor lon,
Anwesa'r bedd yn gyson.

The Grave of David Lloyd George (Earl Dwyfor)

[The rough stone, stone of his heart, is the grave of a man who was a hero to his people; a beauteous watercolour is the merry Dwyfor, t'will ever caress his grave.]

74

Westminster Abbey, London. Winston Churchill (1874–1965) is buried with his wife in Bladon, Oxfordshire.

REMEMBER

WINSTON

CHURCHILL

IN ACCORDANCE WITH THE WISHES OF

THE QUEEN AND PARLIAMENT

THE DEAN & CHAPTER PLACED THIS STONE

ON THE TWENTY FIFTH ANNIVERSARY OF

THE BATTLE OF BRITAIN

15 SEPTEMBER 1965

Arlington Cemetery, Washington, DC, on John F. Kennedy (1917–63).

AND SO, MY FELLOW AMERICANS

ASK NOT WHAT YOUR COUNTRY CAN DO FOR YOU

ASK WHAT YOU CAN DO FOR YOUR COUNTRY

MY FELLOW CITIZENS OF THE WORLD

ASK NOT WHAT AMERICA WILL DO FOR YOU BUT WHAT TOGETHER

WE CAN DO FOR THE FREEDOM OF MAN

South View Cemetery, Atlanta, Georgia.

REV. MARTIN LUTHER KING, Jr.

1929–68

Free at last, free at last
Thank God Almighty
I'm free at last.

**Grange Cemetery, Edinburgh, Scotland.
The 'war' refers to the invasion of Iraq in 2003.**

ROBIN COOK
Parliamentarian and Statesman
Born 28th February 1946
Died 6th August 2005
Beloved husband of
GAYNOR
and much missed father of
CHRIS and PETER

"I may not have succeeded
in halting the war
but I did secure the right of
Parliament to decide on war."

**Warstone Lane Cemetery, Birmingham, on John Baskerville (1706–75),
typographer (partial).**

Stranger
Beneath this cone in unconsecrated ground
A friend to the liberties of mankind directed his body to be inurn'd
May the example contribute to emancipate thy mind.
From the idle fears of Superstition
And the wicked arts of Priesthood.

**St Peter's Cemetery, Nyeri, Kenya. The inscription is followed by the Boy Scout
trail sign (a circle with a dot in the middle) for 'I have gone home'.**

ROBERT BADEN-POWELL
CHIEF SCOUT OF THE WORLD
22ND FEBRUARY 1857
8TH JANURY 1941

OLAVE BADEN-POWELL
WORLD CHIEF GUIDE
22TH FEBURARY 1889
25TH JUNE 1977

Westminster Abbey, London.

1882   1976
Dame Sybil
Thorndike C.H.
wife of
Sir Lewis Casson.
Saint Joan or Hecuba,
great actress of your age,
all womanhood your part,
the world your stage.
To each good cause you lent
your vigorous tongue,
Swept through the years the
champion of the young.
And now the scripts lie fading
on the shelf,
we celebrate your finest
role --- yourself;
The calls, the lights grow dim
but not this part,
The Christian spirit,
the great generous heart.

St Leonard, Shoreditch, London, on James Burbage (1530–97).

THIS STONE IS PLACED HERE
IN THE GLORY OF GOD AND IN AC
KNOWLEDGEMENT OF THE WORK
DONE FOR ENGLISH DRAMA BY THE

PLAYERS MUSICIANS AND OTHER
MEN OF THE THEATRE WHO ARE BU
RIED WITHIN THE PRECINCTS OF THIS
CHURCH AND IN PARTICULAR TO
THE MEMORY OF THOSE WHO
ARE NAMED BELOW
JAMES BURBAGE DIED 1597 A
JOINER BY TRADE AND THE HEAD OF
LORD LEICESTER'S PLAYERS WHO
IN 1576 BUILT IN SHOREDITCH THE
FIRST ENGLISH PLAYHOUSE
THIS HE CALLED THE THEATRE

Southwark Cathedral, London, on which is pictured a drawing of the Globe Theatre.

In thanksgiving for
SAM WANAMAKER CBE
ACTOR
DIRECTOR
PRODUCER
1919–1993
whose vision
rebuilt
Shakespeare's
Globe Theatre
on Bankside
in this
Parish

Golders Green Crematorium, London.

"Life is a state of mind"
WITH EVERLOVING MEMORIES
PETER SELLERS
C.B.E.
1925–1980

Golders Green Crematorium, London.

IVOR NOVELLO
We shall not see
his like again

Strawberry Fields, Central Park, New York, on John Lennon (1940–80).

IMAGINE

Golders Green Crematorium, London.

RONNIE SCOTT
O.B.E.
Jazz Musician
Club Proprietor
Raconteur and Wit.
28th January 1927 –
23rd December 1996.
He was the leader
Of our generation.

Chapter 4

Elegiac, Poignant, & Plaintive

St Nicholas, Islip, Oxfordshire, on William Kent (d. 1640).

As I was so are
Ye, and as I am
So shall ye bee

Said to be in Camberwell, London, on twins.

Richard Wade, died Oct. 21, 1810, aged 53.
Giles Wade, died Dec. 8, 1810, aged 53.

Near together they came,
Near together they went,
Near together they are.

Staunton Harold, Leicestershire, on Sir Robert Shirley (1629–56), a royalist sen to the Tower of London for giving shelter to priests in the church he built.

In the yeare 1653
When all thinges Sacred were throughout the nation
Either demollisht or profaned
Sir Robert Shirley, Barronet
Founded this Church
Whose singular praise it is
To have done the best things in the worst times
And
Hoped them in the most calamitous.
The righteous shall be had in everlasting remembrance.

Concord, Massachusetts.

God wills us free, man wills us slaves.
I will as God wills Gods will be done.
Here lies the body of
JOHN JACK

A native of Africa who died
March 1773, aged about 60 years.

Tho born in a land of slavery,
He was born free.
Tho he lived in a land of liberty,
He lived as a slave,
Till by his honest, tho stolen labors,
He acquired the source of slavery.
Which gave him his freedom,
Tho not long before,
Death the grand tyrant,
Gave him his final emancipation,
And set him on a footing with kings.
Tho a slave to vice,
He practised those virtues,
Without which kings are but slaves.

Rome, first century BCE (tr. from Latin).

GAIUS HOSTIUS PAMPHILUS,
A DOCTOR OF MEDICINE, FREEDMAN OF GAIUS,
BOUGHT THIS MEMORIAL
FOR HIMSELF AND FOR NELPIA HYMNIS,
FREEDWOMAN OF MARCUS;
AND FOR ALL THEIR FREEDMEN AND FREEDWOMEN AND THEIR
POSTERITY THIS FOR EVERMORE IS OUR HOME
THIS IS OUR FARM, THIS OUR GARDENS
THIS OUR MEMORIAL

Said to be in St Mary, Folkstone, Kent.

In memory of
REBECCA ROGERS
who died August 22 1688
Aged 44 years.

A house she hath it's made of such good fashion,
The tenant ne'er shall pay for reparation;

Nor will her landlord ever raise her Rent,
Or turn her out of doors for non-payment;
From chimney money too this Cell is free,
To such a house who would not tenant be.

St Germain's Cathedral (ruins), Peel Castle, Isle of Man, on Dr Samuel Rutter, Bishop of Sodor and Man, said to be self-authored (tr. from Latin).

In this house which I have borrowed from the worms,
my brethren,
Lie I Samuel, by divine permission,
Bishop of this island.
Stop, reader;
Behold and smile at
The Palace of a Bishop!
He died May 30,
In the year 1662.

American Memorial Park Cemetery, Grand Prairie, Dallas County, Texas.

Ricky W. Cross
Oct. 31. 1950
Nov. 20. 1994
Died in America
Land of the homeless

St Mary, Chepstow, Monmouthshire, on Henry Marten, one of the judges who signed Charles I's death warrant and wrote his own epitaph (partial).

Here Sept. 9th 1680,
was buried
A true born Englishman.
Who, in Berkshire was well known
To love his country's freedom like his own,
But being immured full twenty years,
Had time to write as doth appear.

Old North Bridge, Concord, Massachusetts, on soldiers of the 4th King's Own Light Company, who died nearby on 19 April 1775. From a poem by James Russell Lowell (1819–91) of Cambridge, Massachusetts.

GRAVE OF BRITISH SOLDIERS

THEY CAME THREE THOUSAND MILES AND DIED
TO KEEP THE PAST UPON ITS THRONE
UNHEARD BEYOND THE OCEAN TIDE
THEIR ENGLISH MOTHER MADE HER MOAN
APRIL 19 1775

Ridgefield, Connecticut.

IN DEFENSE OF AMERICAN INDEPENDENCE
AT THE BATTLE OF RIDGEFIELD, APR. 27, 1777,
DIED
EIGHT PATRIOTS,
WHO WERE LAID IN THESE GROUNDS,
COMPANIONED BY
SIXTEEN BRITISH SOLDIERS,
LIVING, THEIR ENEMIES: DYING, THEIR GUESTS
IN HONOR OF SERVICE AND SACRIFICE, THIS
MEMORIAL IS PLACED FOR THE
STRENGTHENING OF HEARTS

Washington Square, Philadelphia, Pennsylvania (partial).

FREEDOM IS A LIGHT
FOR WHICH MANY MEN HAVE DIED IN DARKNESS

IN UNMARKED GRAVES WITHIN
THIS SQUARE LIE THOUSANDS
OF UNKNOWN SOLDIERS OF
WASHINGTON'S ARMY WHO DIED
OF WOUNDS AND SICKNESS DURING
THE REVOLUTIONARY WAR

Canterbury Cathedral, Kent.

REMEMBER
THE THOUSANDS OF THE
COMBINED ALLIED FORCES
WHO LOST THEIR LIVES
DURING THE INVASION OF
WESTERN EUROPE
ON THE 6TH OF JUNE 1944
THE ASSAULT ON NORMANDY
WAS LAUNCHED AT SWORD, JUNO
GOLD, OMAHA & UTAH BEACHES
THUS BEGAN THE RETURN
OF-FREEDOM TO EUROPE

Shoreham Aircraft Museum, Sevenoaks, Kent.

IN MEMORY OF GERMAN AIRMEN
OF THE LUFTWAFFE
WHO LOST THEIR LIVES IN
AIR OPERATIONS
OVER THE BRITISH ISLES
BETWEEN OCTOBER 1939
AND MARCH 1945
MÖGEN SIE IN FRIEDEN RUHEN
MAY THEY REST IN PEACE

Greece, for the 300 Spartans killed at the Battle of Thermoplyae, attributed to Simonides of Ceos, c. 480 BCE.

Go, tell the Spartans, you who pass by
That here, obedient to their laws, we lie.

On a plaque in the British War Cemetery on the island of Vis in the Adriatic, by A.E. Housman, composed 1919.

Here we dead lie because we did not choose
To live and shame the land from which we sprung.
Life, to be sure, is nothing much to lose,
But young men think it is, and we were young.

Salisbury Cathedral, Wiltshire.

"When things were at their worst
he would go up and down in the
trenches cheering the men, when
danger was greatest his smile was
loveliest."

In proud and unfading memory of
EDWARD : WYNDHAM : TENNANT
4th Batt. Grenadier Guards, eldest son of Lord and Lady
Glenconner, who passed to the fuller life in the battle of
The Somme 22nd September 1916. Aged 19 years.

He gave his earthly life to such matter as he set great
Store by: the honour of his country and his home

Greece, on the dead in a battle in Boeotia (338 BCE).

O Time, all-surveying deity of the manifold things wrought among
mortals, carry to all men the message of our fate, that striving to
save the holy soil of Greece we die on the renowned Boeotian plains.

On a marble plaque on the isle of Skyros, Greece, where the poet is buried.

RUPERT BROOKE 1887–1915

IF I SHOULD DIE, THINK ONLY THIS OF ME:
THAT THERE'S SOME CORNER OF A FOREIGN FIELD

THAT IS FOR EVER ENGLAND. THERE SHALL BE
IN THAT RICH EARTH A RICHER DUST CONCEALED;
A DUST WHOM ENGLAND BORE, SHAPED, MADE AWARE,
GAVE, ONCE, HER FLOWERS TO LOVE, HER WAYS TO ROAM.
A BODY OF ENGLAND'S, BREATHING ENGLISH AIR.
WASHED BY THE RIVERS, BLEST BY SUNS OF HOME.

AND THINK, THIS HEART, ALL EVIL SHED AWAY,
A PULSE IN THE ETERNAL MIND, NO LESS
GIVES SOMEWHERE BACK THE THOUGHTS BY ENGLAND GIVEN;
HER SIGHTS AND SOUNDS; DREAMS HAPPY AS HER DAY;
AND LAUGHTER, LEARNT OF FRIENDS; AND GENTLENESS,
IN HEARTS AT PEACE, UNDER AN ENGLISH HEAVEN.

St Matthew, Twigworth, Gloucestershire.

Ivor
Gurney
Composer
Poet of the Severn
and
Somme
1890 – 1937

Ypres, France.

SECOND LIEUTENANT
ARTHUR CONWAY YOUNG
ROYAL IRISH FUSILIERS
16TH AUGUST 1917

BORN AT KOBE JAPAN
9TH OCTOBER 1890
SACRIFICED TO THE FALLACY
THAT WAR CAN END WAR

Created for the War Graves Commission by Rudyard Kipling after his son
John was killed in the First World War and used extensively in
two world wars on unidentified soldiers.

A soldier of the Great War.
Known unto God.

Observation Hill, Ross Island, Antarctica, on a wooden cross.
The quotation is from Alfred Tennyson's *Ulysses*.

IN MEMORIAM

CAPT. R.F. SCOTT, R.N.

DR E.A. WILSON, CAPT L.E.G. OATES, INS. DRGS., LT. H.R. BOWERS, R.I.M.

PETTY OFFICER E. EVANS, R.N.

WHO DIED ON THEIR

RETURN FROM THE

POLE. MARCH

1912

TO STRIVE, TO SEEK,

TO FIND,

AND NOT TO

YIELD

St Mary, Gestinghorpe, Essex.

IN MEMORY OF

A VERY GALLANT GENTLEMAN

LAWRENCE EDWARD GRACE OATES

CAPTAIN IN THE INNISKILLING DRAGOONS

BORN MARCH 17 1880 DIED MARCH 17 1912

ON THE RETURN JOURNEY FROM THE SOUTH

POLE OF THE SCOTT ANTARCTIC EXPEDITION

WHEN ALL WERE BESET BY HARDSHIP HE

BEING GRAVELY INJURED WENT OUT INTO

THE BLIZZARD TO DIE IN THE HOPE THAT BY SO

DOING HE MIGHT ENABLE HIS COMRADES TO

REACH SAFETY *** THIS TABLET IS PLACED HERE IN AFFECTIONATE
REMEMBRANCE BY
HIS BROTHER OFFICERS AD 1913

Grytviken, South Georgia. A star is engraved above the inscription. The quotation is on the reverse of the stone.

To the dear
Memory of

ERNEST HENRY
SHACKLETON
EXPLORER

Born 15th Feb 1874
Entered Life Eternal
5th Jan. 1922

"I hold that a
man should strive
to the uttermost
prize"
Robert Browning

Mt Everest, near Rongbuk Base Camp, Tibet, China.

IN MEMORY OF
GEORGE LEIGH MALLORY
& ANDREW IRVINE
LAST SEEN 8TH JUNE 1924
AND ALL THOSE WHO DIED
DURING THE PIONEER
BRITISH MT. EVEREST EXPEDITION

El Alamein, Egypt.

7907008 TROOPER

G. F. GODFREY

THE WARWICKSHIRE YEOMANRY

24TH OCTOBER 1942   AGE 22

TO THE WORLD

HE WAS A SOLDIER

TO ME, HE WAS THE WORLD

Fairview Lawn Cemetery, Halifax, Nova Scotia.

SACRED

TO THE MEMORY OF

EVERETT EDWARD

ELLIOTT

OF THE HEROIC CREW

S.S. "TITANIC" DIED ON DUTY

APRIL 15, 1912

AGE 24 YEARS

EACH MAN STOOD AT HIS POST

WHILE ALL THE WEAKER ONES

WENT BY, AND SHOWED ONCE

MORE TO ALL THE WORLD

HOW ENGLISHMEN SHOULD DIE.

Philharmonic Hall, Hope Street, Liverpool, Merseyside.
The *Titanic* sank on 15 April (not 14).

THIS TABLET IS DEDICATED TO THE MEMORY

OF

W. HARTLEY OF DEWSBURY

"BANDMASTER"

W.T. BRAILEY OF LONDON

R. BRICOUX OF LILLE, FRANCE
J.F. CLARKE OF LIVERPOOL
J.L. HUME OF DUMFRIES
G. KRINS OF LIEGE, BELGIUM
P.C. TAYLOR OF LONDON
J.W. WOODWARD OF HEADINGTON

MEMBERS OF THE BAND ON BOARD
THE "TITANTIC"; THEY BRAVELY
CONTINUED PLAYING TO SOOTHE THE
ANGUISH OF THEIR FELLOW PASSENGERS
UNTIL THE SHIP SANK IN THE DEEP
APRIL 14TH 1912

COURAGE AND COMPASSION JOINED
MAKE THE HERO AND THE MAN COMPLETE

Crematorium, Headington, Oxfordshire.

Remember
HELEN JOY
DAVIDMAN
D. July 1960
Loved wife of
C. S. LEWIS

Here the whole world (stars, water, air,
And field, and forest, as they were
Reflected in a single mind)
Like cast off clothes was left behind
In ashes, yet with hope that she,
Re-born from holy poverty,
In lenten lands, hereafter may
Resume them on her Easter day

Chapter 5

Peculiar, Gothic, Whimsical, & Absurd

St Edmund, Seaton Ross, East Riding of Yorkshire, on William Watson (d. 1857) aged 73, a farmer and self-taught surveyor, cartographer, astronomer, and maker of sundials, who wrote his own epitaph.

At this church I so often with pleasure did call
That I made a sundial upon the church wall.

Elgin Cathedral, Moray, Scotland (a ruin).

Here Lyes
JOHN SHANKS.
Shoemaker in Elgin,
who died 14th April 1841 aged
83 years.
For 17 years he was the keeper, and
the shower of this Cathedral
and while not even the Crown
was doing any thing for its
preservation he, with his own
hands, cleared it of many
thousand cubic yards of rubbish
disclosing the bases of the
pillars, collecting the carved
Fragments, & introducing some
order & propriety

whoso reverences the Cathedral
will respect the memory of
This man.

Ashness Bridge, near Keswick, Cumbria.

IN MEMORY OF
ROBERT GRAHAM PEAKS 1889 – 1966
OF KESWICK
WHO ON THE 13–14 JUNE 1932
TRANSVERSED 42 LAKELAND PEAKS WITHIN 24 HOURS
A RECORD WHICH STOOD FOR 25 YEARS

St Nicholas, Islip, Oxfordshire. A cock, birds, ox, and sheep from Charles Causley's *The Animals Carol* (based on a medieval carol) are carved on the perimeter of the stone, with the corresponding Latin text in a speech bubble before each animal, starting with the cock.

Christus natus est

Quando?
Hoc nocte

In Memory of
Paule Hodgeson
January 16th 1981

Ubi? Ubi?

Bethlehem

returo, nr. Amiternum, Italy, on Protogenes (c. 165–160 BCE?, tr. from Latin).

HERE IS LAID THE JOLLY OLD CLOWN
PROTOGENES, SLAVE OF CLULIUS,
WHO MADE MANY AND MANY
A DELIGHT FOR PEOPLE
BY HIS FOOLING

Minster Church, St Mary the Virgin, Berkeley, Gloucestershire, by Jonathan Swift, who served as chaplain to the Earl of Berkeley, on his fool.

HERE LIES THE EARL OF SUFFOLK'S FOOL,
MEN CALL'D HIM DICKY PEARCE,
HIS FOLLY SERV'D TO MAKE FOLKS LAUGH,
WHEN WIT AND MIRTH WERE SCARCE.
POOR DICK, ALAS IS DEAD AND GONE
WHAT SIGNIFIES TO CRY?
DICKEYS ENOUGH ARE STILL BEHIND,
TO LAUGH AT BY AND BY.
BURIED JUNE 18 MDCCXXVII
AGED 63

St Thomas Becket, Kingsbridge, Devon.

UNDERNEATH
Lieth the Body of ROBERT
Comonly Called BONE PHILLIP
who died July 27th 1793
Aged 63 Years

At whose request the following lines are here inserted
Here lie I at the Chancel door
Here I lie because I'm poor
The farther in the more you'll pay
Here I lie as warm as they.

**Reported as being in Woolwich, Kent. The final couplet
is said to have been added subsequently.**

Youthful reader, passing by,
As you are now, so once was I,
As I am now, so you must be,
Therefore prepare to follow me.

To follow you I am not content,
Until I know which way you went.

Kilkeel, County Down, Northern Ireland.

Here lie the remains of Thomas Nichols
Who died in Philadelphia, March 1753.
Had he lived he would have been buried here.

St Mary, Banbury, Oxfordshire.

To the memory of Ric. Richards, who by a gangrene first lost a Toe,
afterwards a Leg, and lastly his Life on the 7th day of April, 1656.

Ah! cruel Death, to make three Meals of one!
To taste and eat, and Eat 'till all was gone.
But know, thou Tyrant! when the Trump shall call,
He'll find his Feet, and stand when thou shalt fall.

Topsfield, Massachusetts, on Mary Lefavour (d. 1797, partial).
Also, said to be alternatively from Guilford,
Peterborough, and 'a country churchyard'.

Reader, pass on, ne'er waste your time
On bad biography and bitter rhyme;
For what I am, this cumb'rous clay insures,
And what I was, is no affair of yours.

St Mary, Great Witchingham, Norfolk.

In memory of Tho. Alleyn
of Wichingham Magna, Gent:
who died Feb. 3, 1650,
and his 2 wifes

Death here advantage hath of life I spye,
One husband with two wifes at once may lye.

St Leonard, Streatham, London (d. 1746).

Elizabeth, wife of Major General Hamilton, who was married
47 years, and never did one thing to disoblige her Husband.

St Elphin, Warrington, Lancashire, on Margaret Robinson (d. 1816), aged 38.

THIS MAID NO ELEGANCE OF
FORM POSSESSED;
NO EARTHLY LOVE DEFIL'D HER
SACRED BREAST;

HENCE FREE SHE LIV'D FROM
THE DECEIVER MAN;
HEAVEN MEANT IT AS A BLESSING
SHE WAS PLAIN.

St Mary, Wimbledon, London (no longer extant).

Dorothy Cecil unmarried as yet.

St Philip, Birmingham, Warwickshire, England

In memory of Mannetta Stocker,
who quitted this life the fourth day of May,
1819, at the age of thirty-nine years.

The smallest woman in this kingdom,
And one of the most accomplished.
She was not more than thirty-three inches high.
She was a native of Austria.

All Saints, Market Weighton, East Riding of Yorkshire.

In memory of
WILLIAM BRADLEY
SON OF JOHN AND ANN BRADLEY,
OF MARKET WEIGHTON,
WHO DIED MAY 30TH 1820
AGED 33 YEARS.

He Measured
Seven feet nine inches in height
And Weighed
twenty-seven stones.

Christ Church, Skipton, North Yorkshire, on Edwin Calvert (partial).

IN MEMORY OF
THE LATE EDWIN
CALVERT, SON OF
RICHARD CALVERT,
OF SKIPTON (KNOWN BY
THE NAME OF THE
"COMMANDER IN CHIEF" BEING
THE SMALLEST AND MOST
PERFECT MAN IN THE WORLD, BEING
UNDER 36 INCHES IN HEIGHT, AND
WEIGHING 25 LBS.) WHO DIED MUCH
LAMENTED AND DEEPLY REGRETTED
BY ALL WHO KNEW HIM, AUG 7TH
1859, IN THE 17 YEAR OF HIS AGE.

St Michael and All Angels, Great Wolford, Warwickshire.

Here Old John Randall lies,
Who counting from his tale,
Lived three score years and ten,
Such virtue was in Ale.
Ale was his meat,
Ale was his drink,
Ale did his heart revive;
And if he could have drunk his ale,
He still had been alive;
He died January five.
1699.

St Gregory, Turnhill, Dorset, on John Warren, parish clerk (d. 1752).

Here under this stone
Lie Ruth and old John,
Who smoked all his life

And so did his wife:
And now there's no doubt
But their pipes are both out.
Be it said without joke
That life is but smoke;
Though you live to fourscore,
'Tis a whiff and no more.

Providence, Rhode Island, on John Kerr (d. 1835), aged 46, and in numerous other locations. By Peter Patrix, a French poet, composed on the eve of his death.

I dreamt that buried in my fellow clay
Close by a common beggar's side I lay;
Such a mean companion hurt my pride
And like a corpse of consequence I cried:
Scoundrel begone, and henceforth touch me not,
More manners learn, and at a distance rot.
Scoundrel, in still haughtier tones cried he,
Proud lump of earth, I scorn thy words and thee:
All here are equal, they place now is mine;
This is my rotting place, and that is thine.

St Mary, Tetbury, Gloucestershire.

In the Vault underneath
lie several of the SAUNDERSES.
Late of this Parish: – particulars
the last day will disclose.
Amen.

St Lawrence, Church Stretton, Shropshire.

IN MEMORY OF ANN
THE WIFE OF
THOMAS COOK

WHO DIED
JUNE 9TH 1814
AGED 60 YEARS

ON A THURSDAY SHE WAS BORN
ON A THURSDAY MADE A BRIDE
ON A THURSDAY PUT TO BED
ON A THURSDAY BROKE HER LEG, AND
ON A THURSDAY DIED

St Mary, Martham, Norfolk, on Christopher Bunaway (or Burraway), who discovered that he had married his stepmother, Alice Ryall.

Here lyes the body of Christopher Bunaway,
who departed this life ye 18th
day of October, anno domini 1730 aged 59 years.
And there lyes Alice who by her life was
my Sister, my Mistress, my Mother, and my Wife.
Dyed February 12th, 1729 aged 76 years.

Greece, on a favourite dog (c. 350 BCE, tr. from Greek).

You who pass on this path,
If haply you mark this monument,
Laugh not, I pray you, though it is a dog's grave.
Tears fell for me, and the dust was heaped above me
By a master's hand.

Adjacent to Samuel Johnson's House, Gough Square, London.

HODGE
"a very fine cat indeed"
belonging to
SAMUEL JOHNSON (1709–1784)
of Gough Square

Newstead Abbey, Nottinghamshire, on Boatswain, Lord Byron's dog.

Near this Spot
are deposited the Remains of one
Who possessed Beauty without Vanity
Strength without Insolence,
Courage without Ferocity,
and all the Virtues of Man without his Vices.
This praise, which would be unmeaning Flattery,
if inscribed over human Ashes,
is but a just Tribute to the Memory of
BOATSWAIN, a DOG
who was born in Newfoundland, May 1803,
and died at Newstead, Nov. 18, 1808.

Opposite Greyfriars Kirkyard, on Greyfriars Bobby, a Skye terrier who accompanied John Gray, night watchman, on his regular beat.

A TRIBUTE
TO THE AFFECTIONATE FIDELITY OF
GREYFRIARS BOBBY.
IN 1858 THIS FAITHFUL DOG FOLLOWED
THE REMAINS OF HIS MASTER TO GREYFRIARS CHURCHYARD AND LINGERED
NEAR THE SPOT
UNTIL HIS DEATH IN 1872.
WITH PERMISSION
ERECTED BY THE
BARONESS BURDETT COUTTS

Adelaide Cottage, Frogmore, Berkshire.

Here lies DASH
The favourite Spaniel of Her Majesty
Queen Victoria
By whose command this memorial was erected.
He died on the 20th December 1840,

In his ninth year.
His attachment was without selfishness,
His playfulness without malice,
His fidelity without deceit.
Reader,
If you would live beloved and die regretted,
Profit by the example of
DASH.

Ice House Paddock, Stratfield Saye House, on Copenhagen, the horse of Arthur Wellesley, 1st Duke of Wellington.

HERE LIES

COPENHAGEN

THE CHARGER RIDDEN BY

THE DUKE OF WELLINGTON

THE ENTIRE DAY, AT THE

BATTLE OF WATERLOO

BORN 1808 DIED 1836

GOD'S HUMBLER INSTRUMENT, THOUGH MEANER CLAY,

SHOULD SHARE THE GLORY OF THAT GLORIOUS DAY.

Aintree Racecourse, Merseyside, on Red Rum, who won the Grand National three times and twice finished in second place (partial).

RESPECT THIS PLACE

THIS HALLOWED GROUND

A LEGEND HERE

HIS REST HAS FOUND

HIS FEET WOULD FLY

OUR SPIRITS SOAR

HE EARNED OUR LOVE FOR EVERMORE

Sacred to posterity.

In a vault, near this place, lies the body of
ANNE, the only daughter of
EDWARD CHAMBERLAYNE, LL.D.
Born in London, January 20, 1667,
Who,
For a considerable time, declined the matrimonial state,
And scheming many things
Superior to her sex and age,
On 30th of June, 1690,
And under the command of her brother,
With arms and in the dress of a man,
She approv'd herself a true VIRAGO,
By fighting undaunted in a fire ship against the French,
Upwards of six hours
She might have given us a race of heroes,
Had not premature fate interposed.
She returned safe from that naval engagement,
And was married, in some months after, to
JOHN SPRAGGE, Esq,
With whom she lived half a year extremely happy,
But being delivered of a daughter, she died
A few days after,
October 30, 1692.

This monument, to his most dear and affectionate wife, was
Erected by her most disconsolate husband.

**Said to be variously from Horsley-Down, Cumberland, a church in
Northumberland and Horselydown, Bermondsey, London.**

Of Thomas Bond, and Mary his wife,
She was temperate, chaste, and charitable;

But

She was proud, peevish, and passionate.

She was an affectionate wife, and a tender mother;

But

Her husband and child whom she loved,

Seldom saw her countenance, without a disgusting frown;

Wilst she received visitors, whom she despised, with an endearing smile.

Her behaviour was discreet towards strangers,

But

Independent in her family,

Abroad, her conduct was influenced by good breeding;

But

At home, by ill temper,

She was a professed enemy to flattery,

And was seldom known to praise or commend;

But

The talents in which she principally excelled,

Were, difference of opinion, and discovering flaws and imperfections.

She was an admirable economist,

And, without prodigality,

Dispensed plenty to every person in her family;

But

Would sacrifice their eyes to a farthing candle,

She sometimes made her husband happy with her good qualities;

But

Much more frequently miserable - with her many failings;

Insomuch, that in thirty years cohabitation he lamented

That maugre all her virtues,

He had not, in the whole, enjoyed two years of matrimonial comfort.

At Length

Finding that she had lost the affections of her husband,

As well as the regard of her neighbours,

Family disputes having been divulged by servants,

She died of vexation, July 20, 1768,

Aged 48 years.

Her worn out husband survived her 4 months and 2 days,
And departed this life Nov. 28, 1768,
In the 54th year of his age.
William Bond, brother to the deceased, erected this stone,
as a weekly monitor to the surviving wives of this parish,
That they may avoid the infamy
Of having their memories handed to posterity
With a Patch Work character.

St Peter, Bolton-le-Moors, on the celebrated Puritan, John Okey.

JOHN OKEY the servant of God was borne
in London 1608 Came into this Towne 1629
Maried Mary the daughter of James
Crompton of Breightmet 1635 with whom
he lived comfortably 20 yeares & begot
4 sonns and 6 daughters since then he lived
sole till the day of his death In his times
were many Great Changes & terrible
alterations 18 yeares civil wars in
England besides many dreadfull sea
fights The Crown or Command of
England changed 8 times episcopacy
laid aside 14 yeares London burnt by
papists & more stately built againe
Germany wasted 300 miles 200000
protestants murdered in Ireland by
the papists This towne thrice stormed
once taken & plundered He went
thorow many troubles & divers
conditions Found rest joy & happines
only in holines the faith feare & loue
of God in Jesus Christ
He dyed the 29 of Ap & lieth here buried
1684

Come lord Jesus o come quickly

HOLINES IS MANS HAPPINES

Kenosha cemetery, Wisconsin.

OLD BROAD GAUGE

LEWIS KNAPP

Aged   years.

Emigrated
to join his wife and other friends in the celestial
Fields of paradise: thanking God for sense enough
to die as he had lived for thirty years, thoroughly
infidel to all ancient and modern Theological
humbug myths, as taught for fine clothes
and place at others' cost by an
indolent, egotistic, self-elected,
priestly crew.

Columbus City Cemetery, Columbus, Texas on Ike Towell (1849–1934)

HERE RESTS

IKE TOWELL

AN INFIDEL WHO HAD

NO HOPE OF HEAVEN

NOR FEAR OF HELL

WAS FREE OF SUPERSTITION

TO DO RIGHT AND LOVE

JUSTICE WAS HIS RELIGION

St Michael, Macclesfield, on Mary Broomfield.

Dyd 19 Novr, 1755, aged 80
The chief concern of her life for the last
twenty-five years was to order and provide

for her funeral. Her greatest pleasure
was to think and talk about it. She lived
many years on a pension of 9d per week,
and yet she saved £5, which at her own
request was laid out on her funeral.

Alnwick, Northumberland. Mysterious.

Here lieth Martin Elphinston,
Who with his sword did cut in sun-
der the daughter of Sir Harry
Crispe, who did his daughter marry.

She was fat and fulsome;
But men will some-
times eat bacon with their bean,
And love the fat as well as lean.

Maple Grove Old Cemetery, Hoosick Falls, New York.

Ruth Sprague
dau of Gibson
& Elizabeth Sprague.
died June 11, 1846; aged
9 years, 4 months, & 3 days.

She was stolen from the grave
by Roderick R. Clow & dissect
ed at Dr. P.M. Armstrong's office
in Hoosick, N.Y., from which place
her mutilated remains were
obtained & deposited here.

Her body dissected by fiendish Men,
Her bones anatomized,
Her soul, we trust, has risen to God,
Where few Physicians rise.

Woodlawn Cemetery, Bronx, New York, on George Spencer Millet (1894–1909), who worked as an office clerk. An ink eraser is a sharp knife for scraping ink from a paper.

LOST LIFE BY STAB IN FALLING ON
INK ERASER, EVADING SIX YOUNG
WOMEN TRYING TO GIVE HIM
BIRTHDAY KISSES IN OFFICE
OF METROPOLITAN LIFE BUILDING

Pecos Park, Pecos, Texas.

ROBERT CLAY ALLISON
1840–1887
HE NEVER KILLED A MAN
THAT DID NOT NEED KILLING

Boothill Graveyard, Tombstone, Arizona.

HERE
LIES
LESTER MOORE,
FOUR SLUGS
FROM A 44,
NO LESS
NO MORE

Boothill, Arizona, on the George Johnson who it was thought had stolen a horse and was hanged, but later found to have purchased the horse legally.

HERE LIES
GEORGE JOHNSON
HANGED BY
MISTAKE
1882
HE WAS RIGHT

WE WAS WRONG
BUT WE STRUNG
HIM UP
AND NOW HE'S
GONE

Père Lachaise Cemetery, Paris, on the French novelist and performer, Sidonie-Gabrielle Colette.

ICI REPOSE
COLETTE
1873 – 1954
[HERE RESTS COLETTE]

Hollywood Forever Cemetery, Hollywood, California.

JOAN HACKETT
1934–1983
GO AWAY – I'M ASLEEP

Westwood Village Memorial Park, Los Angeles, California, on Jack Lemmon (1925–2001), actor and musician.

Jack Lemmon

in

Westwood Village Memorial Park, Los Angeles, California.

THE BEST IS YET TO COME
FRANCIS ALBERT SINATRA
1915–1998

Westwood Village Memorial Park, Los Angeles, California, on Billy Wilder (1906–2002), filmmaker, screenwriter, producer, artist, and journalist. The quotation is the final line from Wilder's film *Some Like It Hot*.

BILLY WILDER
I'M A WRITER
BUT THEN
NOBODY'S PERFECT

Westwood Memorial Park, Los Angeles, California, on Rodney Dangerfield (Jacob Cohen), comedian, actor (1921–2004).

Rodney
Dangerfield
There goes the neighborhood.

Sigourney, Keokuk County, Iowa.

Edward Russell Gann
Jul. 19, 1917 – Nov. 10, 1983

"I'd rather be in Acapulco!"

Oakland Cemetery, Warren, Pennsylvania.

DEWEY HILL
1899 – 1938

SURE HOPE IT'S BETTER WHERE YOU
WENT THEN WHERE YOU'VE BEEN
A.H. HILL - SON – 1982

Mount Pleasant Cemetery, Toronto, Ontario, Canada.

HOWARD W.
JANNACK

1926–2004

LOVER OF LITTLE UGLY DOGS

Saint Francis De Sales Cemetery, Lenni, Pennsylvania.

ELIZABETH M.

MARKUNAS

1932–1993

"NOBODY EVER LISTENED

TO ME"

Sallee Cemetery, Gainesville, Missouri.

JOHN P MCKEE

DEC 16 1913

OCT 7 1989

CAUSE OF DEATH

REAGANOMICS

Cedar Hill Cemetery, Vicksburg, Mississippi.

THOMAS M. MORRISEY

MAY 4, 1929

MAR. 14, 1985

ADVERSE TO THE PLOW

PRONE TO THE FIDDLE AND JUG

Yarmouth Ancient Cemetery, Massachusetts.

MARY C. DOLENCIE

1906–1995

MAY ETERNAL DAMNATION BE

UPON THOSE IN WHALING PORT

WHO, WITHOUT KNOWING ME,

HAVE MALICIOUSLY VILIFIED ME.

MAY THE CURSE OF GOD

BE UPON THEM AND THEIRS.

Beth David Memorial Gardens, Hollywood, Florida. Mr Harband was not buried at Beth David Memorial Gardens but owned a plot there and erected this stone thereon. It was removed in 2004.

HERMAN HARBAND

1918

MY WIFE ELEANOR ARTHUR

OF QUEENS, NY LIVED LIKE

A PRINCESS FOR 20 YEARS

TRAVELING THE WORLD WITH

THE BEST OF EVERYTHING.

WHEN I WENT BLIND

SHE TRIED TO POISON ME,

TOOK ALL MY MONEY,

ALL MY MEDICATION AND

LEFT ME IN THE DARK

ALONE AND SICK.

IT'S A MIRACLE I ESCAPED.

I WON'T SEE HER IN HEAVEN

BECAUSE SHE'S SURELY

GOING TO HELL!

Mount Moriah Cemetery, Withamsville, Ohio

JOSEPH PASTY ORSE

HE DIED BECAUSE OF HIS WIFE

9 – 16 – 73

St Thomas, Winchelsea, East Sussex. The Gaelic inscription (Milligan held an Irish passport) was necessary to secure the consent of the Diocese of Chichester.

love, light, peace
Terence Alan
(Spike)
Milligan c.b.e., k.b.e.
1918 – 2002

writer artist musician
humanitarian, comedian

Duirt mé leat go raibh mé breoite
[I told you I was ill]

Reeds Lake Cemetery, Temple, Texas.

HARRIS
GEORGE W. JR
MAY 31, 1927

I KNEW THIS WOULD HAPPEN

Chapter 6

Violent or Untimely Death

Stanton Harcourt, Oxfordshire, on a young couple killed by lightning a week before their marriage. At the time, Alexander Pope was staying at Stanton Harcourt and composed the following epitaph.

NEAR THIS PLACE LIE THE BODIES OF

JOHN HEWET AND SARAH DREW

AN INDUSTRIOUS YOUNG MAN

AND VIRTUOUS YOUNG MAIDEN OF THIS PARISH;

CONTRACTED IN MARRIAGE

WHO BEING WITH MANY OTHERS AT HARVEST

WORK WERE IN ONE INSTANT KILLED

BY LIGHTNING ON THE LAST DAY OF JULY

1718

Think not by rigorous judgment seized
A pair so faithful could expire;
Victims so pure, Heaven saw well pleased.
And snatched them in eternal fire.
Live well, and fear no sudden fate;
When God calls victims to the grave,
Alike 'tis justice soon or late
Mercy alike to kill or save.
Virtue unmoved can hear the Call,
And face the flash that melts the Ball.

All Saints, Ockham, Surrey.

The Lord saw good, I was topping off wood,
And down fell from the tree;
I met with a check, and I broke my blessed neck,
And so Death topped off me.

Howard Street Cemetery, Salem, Massachusetts.

In Memory of
Captain Samuel Skerry Junr.

Of Brookfield formerly of
this Town while here on
a visit on Saturday between
4 & 5 oclock PM in Mr. Pope's
Stable viewing a span of
Horses he was suddenly kicked
by one of them in the lower
part of his Bowels & departed
this life on Sunday evening
Oct. 23, 1808. Æt. 36

St Mary, Swaffham Bulbeck, Cambridgeshire.

Sacred to the Memory of
ALFRED RULE
who died in the 12th year of his age,
a few hours after both his legs had been broken by the wheels of a cart
passing over them with a runaway horse.
August 18 1870
In the midst of life we are in death.

Postman's Park, London.

WILLIAM DRAKE

LOST HIS LIFE IN AVERTING A

SERIOUS ACCIDENT TO A LADY

IN HYDE PARK

APRIL 2 1869

WHOSE HORSES WERE UNMANAGEABLE

THROUGH THE BREAKING

OF THE CARRIAGE POLE.

Postman's Park, London.

FREDERICK ALFRED CROFT

INSPECTOR. AGED 31

SAVED A LUNATIC WOMAN
FROM SUICIDE AT WOOLWICH
ARSENAL STATION BUT WAS
HIMSELF RUN OVER BY THE TRAIN
JAN 11 1878

Old First Parish, Rockport, Massachusetts.

In Memory of
Capt. Samuel Davis Esq.
Ruling Elder in the Church
Obt. August 25th 1770
Aged 67

Four Sons lost at Sea
Ebenezer 1746 Aged 21
Samuel 1759 Aged 32
William 1759 Aged 21
Henry 1766 Aged 24

Old Burial Hill, Plymouth, Massachusetts.

James Jordan. Drowned in Smelt Pond, June 25, 1837, aged 27 y'rs.
Buried on the day he was to have been married.

Postman's Park, London.

WILLIAM DONALD OF
BAYSWATER, AGED 19
RAILWAY CLERK
WAS DROWNED IN THE LEA
TRYING TO SAVE A LAD FROM A
DANGEROUS ENTANGLEMENT OF
WEED   JULY 16 1876

St James the Great, Radley, Oxfordshire,
on Lt Colonel William Bowyer (d. 1808).

High in his Profession
brave, honourable & universally beloved:
all his prospects in life seemed Bright & Flattering.
when it pleased Almighty God
that he should fall a victim to the Climate
of the West Indies.

Exeter Cathedral, Devon.

Sacred to the Memory
of RACHEL CHARLOTTE O'BRIEN,
Wife of Captn E. J. O'BRIEN,
of His Majesty's 24th Reg.mt
and daughter of JOS. FROBISHER, Esq.,
of Montreal, Canada.
Her Death was occasioned by
her Clothes catching Fire;
seeing the flames
communicating to her Infant,
all Regard to her own Safety,
was lost in the
more powerful Consideration
of saving her Child,
and rushing
out of the Room, she
preserved its Life, at the
Sacrifice of her own.
She expired on the 13th Dec.
A.D. 1800,
in the 19th Year of her Age.

St Mary, Stoke Newington, London.

This tomb was erected by William Picket,
of the City of London, Goldsmith,
on the melancholy death of his daughter
ELIZABETH

A testimony of respect from greatly afflicted parents;
In memory of ELIZABETH PICKET, Spinster
Who died December 11th, 1781
Aged 23 years.

This much lamented young person expired
in consequence of her cloaths taking fire
the preceding evening.

Reader, if ever you should witness such
an affecting scene, recollect that the only method to
extinguish the flame is to stifle it by an immediate covering.

St Andrew, Soham, Cambridgeshire.

This tablet commemorates the heroic action of
Fireman J.W. Nightall G.C. who gave his life &
Driver B Gimbert G.C. who was badly injured
whilst detaching a blazing wagon from an
Ammunition train at Soham station at 1.43am
June 2nd 1944. The station was totally destroyed &
considerable damage was done by the explosion
The devotion to duty of these brave men saved
the town of Soham from grave destruction
Signalman Bridges was killed whilst on duty &
Guard H Clarke suffered from shock

Be strong and quit yourselves like men.

St Cuthbert, Marton-in-Cleveland, Middlesbrough, on three men who hid a stolen beef in a cave, intending later to retrieve it.

ected in memory of Robert Armstrong aged 28, James Ingledew aged 39 d Joseph Fenison aged 27 years who unfortunately lost their lives Oct 11th 12 by venturing into a well at Marton when it was filled with carbonic acid s or fixed air. From this unhappy accident let others take warning not to nture into wells without first trying whether a candle will burn in them; the candle burns to the bottom they may enter with safety, if it goes out man life cannot be supported.

Salem, Massachusetts (partial).

In Memory of
MR. ABNER HILL
whose Death was caused by
his falling from a building when
employ'd in the business of life
Oct. 25 1806
Aged 23 Years.

Dornoch, Highlands, Scotland, in a remote area east of the town on the edge of a wood. Such was the stigma attached to cholera that the stone contains a denial.

ERECTED
BY K.R.
over the remains
of his dutiful Father
K.R. who departed this
life July 24 1832 aged 44
years. It was then suppo
sed he died of cholera
but afterwards contra
dicted by most eminent
medical men.

SS Peter and Paul, Wantage, Oxfordshire.

Between this Wall and the pathway
Were interred from Sept 29th to Oct 13th
1832 the bodies of sixteen persons,
who with three others of this Town
had died of the Asiatic Cholera,
the ravages of which disease were
mercifully terminated by Him who
alone could say to the Angel of the
Pestilence- "It is enough, stay
Now thine hand.'

RESTORED NOV. 1960

Howard Street Cemetery, Salem, Massachusetts.

In Memory of
Mr. LUTHER MORGAN
Son of
Lucas Morgan Esq;
of West Springfield,
who died of a Pulmonary
Consumption while on a
visit to his friends in this
Town Jan. 29, 1808

Bunhill Fields, London. Dame Mary Page (1672–1728), believed to have suffered from Meigs' syndrome, underwent numerous treatments to drain off excess fluid from her body.

Here Lyes DAME MARY PAGE,
Relict of Sir Gregory Page, Bart.
She departed this life March 4 1728,
in the 56th year of her age.

In 67 months she was tap'd 60 times
had taken away 240 gallons of water

without ever repining at her case
or ever fearing the operation.

Plymouth, Massachusetts.

To the memory of Miss Hanna Howland
Who died of a Languishment
January ye 27th 1780 Ætatis 26.

For us they languish, & for us they die,
And shall they languish, shall they die in vain?

St Andrew, Bramfield, Suffolk.

Beneath the remains of her Brother Edward
of her Husband Arthur
Here lies the Body of Bridgett Applethwait
Once Bridgett Nelson.
After the fatigues of a Married Life,
Born by her with Incredible Patience,
For four years and three Quarter, bating three weeks;
And after the Enjoiment of the Glorious Freedom
Of an Easy and Unblemisht Widowhood,
For four years and upwards,
She resolved to run the Risk of a second Marriage-Bed
But DEATH forbad the Banns,
And having with an Apopleptick Dart
(The same instrument with which he had Formerly
Dispatch't her Mother)
Touch't the most Vital part of her Brain;
She must have fallen Directly to the Ground
(as one Thunder-strook)
If she had not been Catch't and Supported
by her Intended Husband,
Of which Invisible Bruise,
After a Struggle for above sixty hours,

With that Grand Enemy of Life
(But the certain and Merciful Friend to Helpless Old Age)
In Terrible Convulsions, Plaintive Groans, or Stupefying Sleep
without recovery of her speech or senses,
She Dyed on the 12th day of Sep: in ye year
of Our Lord 1737 and of her own Age 44.

Rebecca Nurse Homestead, Danvers, Massachusetts, on the only victim of the Salem witch trials whose body was identified and whose burial site is proven. Initially buried in secret in Danvers, Massachusetts, his body was unearthed when it was disturbed by builders and reburied in 1992.

HERE LYES BURIED

THE BODY OF

GEORGE JACOBS SR

DECD AUGUST THE 19

1692

WELL! BURN ME, OR HANG ME,

I WILL STAND IN THE TRUTH

OF CHRIST.

Rougemont Castle, Exeter, Devon.

THE DEVON WITCHES
In memory of
Temperance Lloyd
Susannah Edwards
Mary Trembles
of Bideford, died 1682
Alice Molland
DIED 1685
THE LAST PEOPLE IN ENGLAND
TO BE EXECUTED FOR WITCHCRAFT
TRIED HERE & HANGED AT HEAVITREE
In the hope of an end to persecution & intolerance.

Near the Bridge of St Bartholomew, Rome (c. 135–120 BCE),
on Claudia (tr. from Latin).

Stranger, my message is short. Stand by and read it through.
Here is the unlovely tomb of a lovely woman.
Her parents called her Claudia by name.
She loved her husband with her whole heart.
She bore two sons; of these she leaves one on earth;
under the earth has she placed the other.
She was charming in converse, yet proper in bearing.
She kept house, she made wool. That's my last word. Go your way.

St Paul, Bedford, Bedfordshire.

Patience, wife of SHADRACH JOHNSON
The mother of 24 children, and died in childbed,
June 6, 1717.
Shadrach! Shadrach!
The Lord granted unto thee
Patience,
Who laboured long and patiently
In her vocation;
But her patience being exhausted,
She departed in the midst of her labour,
Aetat. 38.
May she rest from her labours.

Said to be in Meigle, Perth, to William Anderson's children, 1732.

While old grey heads escape the rage
Of cruel death, sometime
Young ones, alas ! may quit the stage,
Ev'n in their very prime.

Oh, death how fierce thy firy Blows,
Nor forrester like thee;

Cuts down the cedar while it grows
And spares the weathered tree.

Salem, Massachusetts.

Three infant
daughters of Capt.
Timothy & Lydia
Paige each named
Hannah died June
11, 1776: Oct. 17, 1777:
June 15, 1782.

Old Burial Hill, Marblehead, Massachusetts. On four, conjoined tombstones, for children of the same family.

Richard Stivens, Who died July 18 1756, Aged 4 mos & 18 Days.	A Child Who died the Same Day She was born June 10 1757	Richard Stivens Who died July 18 1758 Aged 1 year & 11 Months	Margaret Stivens Who died Octob 21 1759. Aged 1 Month

God takes the good too good on earth to stay,
And leave's the bad too bad to take away.

Said to be in Leeds Minster, Yorkshire.

Under this stone do lie six children small,
Of John Wittington of the North Hall.
Mors omnibus communis.
[Death is common to all]

Nevern, Pembrokeshire, on Anna, Letitia and George, infant children of the Rev. D. Griffith, vicar (1783–1834) (partial).

They tasted of Life's bitter cup;
And did not drink their portion up;

They turned their little head aside
Disgusted with the taste _ and died.

To the memory of Mary Morgan,
who young and beautiful, endowed
with a good understanding and
disposition, but unenlightened by the
sacred truths of Christianity become
the victim of sin and shame and
was condemned to an ignominious
death on the 11th April 1805,
for the Murder of her bastard Child.

Rous'd to a first sense of guilt and
remorse by the eloquent and humane
exertions of her benevolent Judge,
Mr. Justice Hardinge, she underwent
the Sentence of the Law on the
following Thursday with unfeigned
repentance and a furvent hope of
forgiveness through the merits of a
                    redeeming intercessor.
This stone is erected not merely to
perpetuate the remembrance of a
departed penitent, but to remind the
living of the frailty of human nature
when unsupported by Religion.

St Mary, Godmanchester, Cambridgeshire.

As a Warning
To the Young of both Sexes
This Stone is erected by public Subscription
over the remains of MARY ANN WEEMS
who at an early age became acquainted
with THOMAS WEEMS formerly of this Parish
this connextion terminating in a compulsory
Marriage occasioned him soon to desert her
and wishing to be Married to another Woman
he filled up the measure of his iniquity
by resolving to murder his Wife
which he barbarously perpetrated at Wendy
on their Journey to London toward which place
he had induced her to go under the mask
of reconciliation May the 7th 1819
He was taken within a few hours after
the crime was committed, tried and
subsequently executed at Cambridge
on the 7th of August in the same Year

Ere Crime you perpetrate survey this Stone
Learn hence the God of Justice sleeps not on his Throne
But marks the Sinner with unerring Eye
The suffering Victim hears and makes the Guilty die

Old North Church, Boston, Massachusetts.

Major John Pitcairn
Fatally wounded
while rallying the Royal Marines
at the Battle of Bunker Hill
was carried from the field to the boats
on the back of his son
who kissed him and returned to duty.

He died June 17, 1775 and his body
was interred beneath this church.

Greenwood Cemetery, Saint Albans, Vermont.

JOSEPH PARTRIDGE BRAINERD,
SON OF JOSEPH H. BRAINERD
and his wife Fanny Partridge, a
conscientious, faithful, brave,
Union Soldier, was born on the
27th day of June 1840, graduated
from the University of Vermont in
August 1862, enlisted into Co. I
of the Vermont Cavalry, was
wounded and taken prisoner by
the Rebels in the Wilderness, May
5, 1864, was sent to Andersonville
Prison Pen in Georgia where he
died on the 11th day of September
1864, entirely and wholly
neglected by President Lincoln
and murdered with impunity by
the Rebels, with thousands of our
loyal Soldiers by Starvation, Pri-
vation, Exposure and Abuse.

t Mary, Hunstanton, Norwich, on William Webb of the 15th Light Dragoons.

I am not dead, but sleepeth here,
And when the trumpet sound I will appear.
Four balls through me pierced their way,
Hard it was, I had no time to pray.
The stone that here you do see
My comrades erected for the sake of me.

All Saints, Southill, Bedfordshire. On Admiral Byng (1704–57), who was shot for failing to do 'his utmost' to retake Menorca for the British.

To the perpetual Disgrace
of public Justice,
The Honourable JOHN BYNG,
Admiral of the Blue,
Fell a Martyr to
Political Persecution,
On 14th March in the year 1757,
When Bravery and Loyalty
Were insufficient Securities
For the Life and Honour
Of a Naval Officer.

St Mary, Beverley, East Riding of Yorkshire, on a memorial plaque which shows two crossed duelling swords.

Here two young Danish Soldiers lye
The one in quarrel chanced to die;
The others Head by their own Law,
With Sword was sever'd at one Blow.
December 23d
1689

St George, York,

JOHN PALMER OTHERWISE
RICHARD TURPIN
THE NOTORIOUS HIGHWAYMAN AND HORSE STEALER
EXECUTED AT TYBURN, APRIL 17TH, 1739
AND BURIED IN ST. GEORGES CHURCHYARD

St Michael and All Angels, Thursley, Surrey, on an unknown solider who was walking from London to Portsmouth to join his ship. Stopping at a pub, he paid for the food and drink of three fellow sailors whom he met, James Marshall, Michael Casey, and Edward Lonegon. They joined him on the walk, where they attacked and murdered him, stealing his purse and effects. Having tried to sell the sailor's clothes, they were arrested, tried, convicted, and hanged.

In Memory of
A generous but unfortunate Sailor,
Who was barbarously murder'd at Hindhead
on Sep. 24th 1786,
By three Villains,
After he had liberally treated them,
And promised them farther Assistance,
On the road to Portsmouth.

When pitying Eyes to see my grave shall come
And with a generous Tear bedew my Tomb
Here shall they read my melancholy Fate.
With Murder and Barbarity complete.
In perfect Health, and in Flow'r of Age,
I fell a Victim to three Ruffians Rage,
On bended knees I mercy strove t'obtain.
Their Thrist of Blood made all Entreaties vain.
No dear Relation, or still dearer Friend
Weeps my hard Lot, or miserable End;
Yet o'er my sad Remains (my name unknown)
A generous Public have inscrib'd this Stone.

St Paul, Hammersmith, London.

HERE

LIE INTERRED THE MORTAL REMAINS

OF

RICHARD HONEY

CARPENTER, AGED 36 YEARS,

AND OF
GEORGE FRANCIS,
BRICKLAYER, AGED 43 YEARS,
WHO WERE SLAIN ON THE 14TH AUGUST, 1821,
WHILE ATTENDING
THE FUNERAL OF
CAROLINE, OF BRUNSWICK,
QUEEN OF ENGLAND.

THE DETAILS OF THAT MELANCHOLY EVENT
BELONG TO THE HISTORY OF THE COUNTRY
IN WHICH THEY WILL BE RECORDED
TOGETHER WITH THE PUBLIC OPINION
DECIDEDLY EXPRESSED RELATIVE TO THE
DISGRACEFUL TRANSACTIONS
OF THAT DISASTROUS DAY
DEEPLY IMPRESSED WITH THEIR FATE
UNMERITED AND UNAVENGED
THEIR RESPECTIVE TRADES INTERRED THEM
AT THEIR GENERAL EXPENCE
ON THE 24TH OF THE SAME MONTH
AND ERECTED THIS STONE
TO THEIR MEMORY.

RICHARD HONEY LEFT ONE FEMALE ORPHAN.
GEORGE FRANCIS LEFT A WIDOW AND THREE YOUNG CHILDREN.

VICTIMS LIKE THESE HAVE FALLEN IN EVERY AGE
STRETCH OF POW'R OR PARTY'S CRUEL RAGE
UNTIL EVEN HANDED JUSTICE COMES AT LAST
TO AMEND THE FUTURE AND AVENGE THE PAST
THEIR FRIENDS AND FELLOW-MEN LAMENT THEIR DOOM
PROTECT THEIR ORPHANS, AND ERECT THEIR TOMB.

Winchester Cathedral, Hampshire.

In Memory of
<small>THOMAS THATCHER</small>
a Grenadier in the Ninth Regiment
of Hants Militia, who died of a
violent Fever contracted by drinking
Small Beer when Hot the 12th of May
1769, Aged 26 Years.
In grateful remembrance of whose Universal
Good will towards his Comrades, this Stone
is placed here at their expense as a small
testimony of their regard and concern.
Here sleeps in peace a Hampshire grenadier,
Who caught his death by drinking cold small beer;
Soldiers beware, from his untimely fall,
And, when ye're hot, drink strong or none at all.

This Stone was replaced by the North Hants
Militia when disembodied at Winchester
on 26th April 1802. in consequence of
the original Stone being destroyed.

And again replaced by
The Royal Hampshire Regiment 1966.

St Mary the Virgin, Morpeth, Northumberland. Emily Davison, a militant suffragette was arrested on several occasions. She threw herself before King George V's horse at the Epsom Derby and died four days later of her injuries. The final line was the motto of the suffragettes.

GREATER LOVE HATH NO MAN
THAN THIS, THAT A MAN LAY
DOWN HIS LIFE FOR HIS FRIENDS

EMILY WILDING
DAVISON
BORN OCT 11TH 1872
DIED JUNE 8TH 1913

DEEDS NOT WORDS

St Mary, St Mary's Street, Shrewsbury.

Let this small Monument record the name
Of CADMAN, and to future times proclaim
How by'n attempt to fly from this high spire
Across the Sabrine stream he did acquire
His fatal end. 'Twas not for want of skill
Or courage to perform the task he fell:
No, no, a faulty Cord being drawn too tight
Hurried his Soul on high to take her flight
Which bid the Body here beneath good Night:
Febry 2nd 1739 aged 28.

All Saints, Pocklington, East Riding of Yorkshire.

IN
MEMORY OF
THOMAS PELLING,
Burton Stather, Lincolnshire,
commonly called 'The Flying Man',
who was killed against the Battlement of
Ye choir when coming down a rope from
the steeple of this church.
This fatal accident happened on the
10TH April, he was buried on the 16TH April 1733,
Exactly under the place where he died.

Holy Trinity, Milton Regis, Kent, on one who it seems perished in the celebrations on Guy Fawkes night.

HERE lyeth the
body of SIMON
GILKER Junior
who was killed by
means of a Rockett
November 5, 1696
AGED 48 Years.
Also the body of Elizabeth his wife

Malmesbury Abbey, Wiltshire, on Hannah Twynnoy, a barmaid at the White Lion Inn, who died after she was attacked by a wild animal belonging to a travelling menagerie.

In memory of
Hannah Twynnoy
Who died October 23rd 1703
Aged 33 Years.

In bloom of Life
She's snatched from hence,
She had not room to make defence;
For Tyger fierce
Took Life away.
And here she lies
In a bed of Clay,
Until the Resurrection Day.

Burn of Lyth, Bower, Caithness, Scotland.

IN MEMORIAM
THIS MEMORIAL IS TO HONOUR AND COMMEMORATE
ALL RANKS OF THE ROYAL ENGINEER COMMANDOS,
AMRY AND ROYAL AUSTRALIAN AIR FORCE GLIDER

PILOTS, THE AIRCREW OF HALIFAX "B" BAKER
NO W7801, WHO PERISHED IN NORWAY
TAKING PART IN OPERATION FRESHMAN.

THIS MISSION WAS TO DESTROY THE VITAL SOURCE OF
HEAVY WATER PRODUCTION AT VERMOK NORWAY THUS
TEMPORARILY PREVENTING GERMAN ATOMIC RESEARCH.

'OPERATION FRESHMAN' COMMENCED ON THE NIGHT
OF 19TH NOVEMBER 1942 BY TWO "HORSA" GLIDERS
TOWED BY HALIFAX BOMBERS FROM R.A.F. SKITTEN
CAITHNESS. ONE HALIFAX ALONE RETURNED.

"VIVIL HUSKE DEM"
THE PRICE THAT WAS PAID
WE WILL ALWAYS REMEMBER
EVERY DAY EVERY MONTH NOT JUST NOVEMBER.

Northmavine, Shetland, Scotland.

M.S.

DONALD ROBERTSON,
Born 1st January 1758; died 4th June 1848
Aged 63 years
He was a peaceable quiet man, and to
all appearance a sincere Christian.
His death was very much regretted
which was caused by the stupidity of
Laurence Tulloch, of Clotherton, who
sold him nitre instead of Epsom salts, by
which he was killed in the space of 3
hours after taking a dose of it.

St Margaret, Wolstanton, Staffordshire, on Sarah Smith (d. 1736)

> It was C—s B—w
> That brought me to my end.
> Dear parents, mourn not for me
> For God will stand my friend
> With half a Pint of Poyson
> He came to visit me.
> Write this on my Grave
> That all that read it may see.

Said to be in St Leonard, Eynsham, Oxfordshire, on a family which perished most likely as a result of the Great Plague (the last major epidemic of bubonic plague to occur in England).

> E. G. Hancock, died August 3, 1666.
> John Hancock, Sen.   ---- 4, ----
> John Hancock, Jun.   ---- 7, ----
> Oner Hancock,   ---- 7, ----
> William Hancock,   ---- 7, ----
> Alice Hancock,   ---- 9, ----
> Ann Hancock,   ---- 10, ----

Chapter 7

Literary Epitaphs

Said to have been on Alexander the Great.

A tomb now suffices him for whom the whole world was not sufficient.

**On Robert Dudley (1532–88), the Earl of Leicester,
attributed to Sir Walter Raleigh.**

> here lyes the noble warryor
> that never bludyed sword
> her lyes the noble courtier
> that never kept his woord
>
> Her lyes his excellency
> that governs all the state
> her lyes the Earl of Leicester
> that all the world did hate.

On Richard Burbage (1568–1619), actor and colleague of William Shakespeare

Exit Burbage

**John Wilmot, 2nd Earl of Rochester (1647–80), on Charles II (1630–85)
(mutton=courtesan).**

> Here lies our mutton-eating king,
> Whose word no man relies on;
> He never said a foolish thing,
> And never did a wise one.

The king is alleged to have replied: 'This is very true: for my words are my own, and my actions are my ministers.'

**On Thomas Fuller (1608–61), author of *The History of the Worthies of England*
as he proposed.**

Here lies Fuller's Earth.

In the same vein, on William Walker (1623–84), author of
A Treatise Of English Particles, 1655.

Here lies Walker's particles.

Johannes Kepler's (mathematician, astronomer, 1571–1630) suggested epitaph
for himself (tr. from Latin).

I measured the skies, now the shadows I measure
Skybound was the mind, earthbound the body rests.

John Gay (1685–1732), dramatist, used on his tombstone in Westminster Abbey.

Life is a jest, and all things show it;
I thought so once; and now I know it.

On Sir John Vanburgh (1664–1726), poet and architect by Abel Evans
(1679–1737). Among Vanburgh's best known buildings are
Blenheim Palace and Castle Howard.

Under this stone, Reader, survey
Dead Sir John Vanbrugh's house of clay.
Lie heavy on him, Earth! for he
Laid many heavy loads on thee!

Soame Jenyns' (1704–87) epitaph on Dr Johnson (1709–84).

Here lies poor Johnson. Reader! have a care,
Tread lightly, lest you rouse a sleeping bear.
Religious, moral, generous and humane,
He was, but self-conceited, rude and vain:
Ill-bred, and overbearing in dispute,
A scholar and a Christian, yet a brute.
Would you know all his wisdom and his folly,
His actions, sayings, mirth, and melancholy,
Boswell and Thrale, retailers of his wit,
Will tell you how he wrote, and talked, and spit.

On Samuel Foote (1720–77), actor, dramatist, and comedian.

Here lies one Foote, whose death may thousands save,
For death has now one foot within his grave.

Robert Burns (1759–96) on William Michie, schoolmaster of Cleish Parish.

Here lie Willie Michie's banes;
O Satan, when ye tak him,
Gie him the schulin o' your weans,
For clever deils he'll mak them!

On David Hume (1711–76), attributed to George Barclay.

Within this circular idea
Called vulgarly a tomb,
The ideas and impressions lie
That constituted Hume

On Patrick Robertson (1794–1855), by John Gibson Lockhart (1794–1854).

Here lies that peerless paper peer Lord Peter
Who broke the laws of God and man and metre.

Benjamin Franklin's (1706–90) suggested epitaph for himself.

The body of Benjamin Franklin, Printer,
Like the cover of an old book
its contents torn out,
and stripped of its lettering and gilding,
lies here, food for worms.
But the work shall not be wholly lost,
for it will, as he believed, appear once more,
in a new and more perfect edition,
corrected and amended
by the Author.

Frederick, Prince of Wales (1707–51), heir apparent till his death, was estranged from his father George III.

> Here lies Fred
> who was alive and is dead,
> Had it been his father
> I had much rather,
> Had it been his sister
> nobody would have missed her,
> Had it been his brother,
> Still better than another,
> Had it been the whole generation,
> So much better for the nation,
> But since it is Fred
> Who was alive and is dead,
> There is no more to be said!

Alexander Pope's suggested epitaph for Isaac Newton.

> Nature and Nature's Laws lay hid in Night:
> God said, 'Let Newton be!' and all was Light.

Alexander Pope, 'For One Who Would Not Be Buried in Westminster Abbey'.

> HEROES and KINGS! your distance keep;
> In peace let one poor Poet sleep,
> Who never flatter'd folks like you:
> Let Horace blush, and Virgil too.

Lord Byron (1788–1824) on the statesman Robert Stewart, Viscount Castlereagh (1769–1822). He was Chief Secretary for Ireland when the Irish Rebellion of 1798 was suppressed and played a leading part in the creation of the Irish Act of Union of 1800.

> Posterity will ne'er survey a nobler grave than this:
> Here lie the bones of Castlereagh: Stop, traveler, and piss!

Pierce Egan (1772–1849) on John Small (1737–1826), one of the greatest cricket batsman of the eighteenth century, from his *Book of Sports And Mirror of Life: Embracing the Turf, the Chase, the Ring, and the Stage.*

Here lies, bowled out by Death's unerring ball,
A Cricketer renowned, by name John Small.
But though his name was Small, yet great his fame,
For nobly did he play the noble game ;
His life was like his innings, long and good,
Full ninety summers he had death withstood,
At length the ninetieth winter came, when (fate
Not leaving him one solitary mate)
This last of Hambledonians, old John Small,
Gave up his bat and ball, his leather, wax, and all.

Epitaph on a dog, 1747, in the style of Alexander Pope.

Here lies a pattern for the human race,
A dog who did his work and knew his place:
A trusty Servant, to his master dear,
A good companion, and a friend sincere.
In spite of bribes and threats, severely just;
He sought no pension, and he broke no trust.
The midnight thief and strolling gypsie found
That faithful Sancho watch'd the mansion round ...

Truth warm'd his breast, and love without disguise,
His heart was grateful, and his actions wise.
In him, through life, all social virtues shone;
– May no rude hands disturb his peaceful grave
For nature's gifts to use in nature's way
Is all the duty beast or man can pay.

From George Macdonald's *David Elginbrod* (1862).

> Here lie I, Martin Elginbrodde:
> Have mercy o' my soul, Lord God,
> As I wad do, were I Lord God
> And ye were Martin Elginbrodde.

On William Buckland, DD FRS (1784–1856), one of the greatest eccentrics of the nineteenth century. Dean of Westminster Abbey and Reader in Geology in the University of Oxford, he wrote the first full account of a fossil dinosaur.

Mourn, ammonites, mourn o'er his funeral urn
    Whose neck ye must grace no more;
Gneiss, Granite, and Slate! he settled your date,
    And his ye must now deplore.

Weep, Caverns, weep! with infiltering drip,
    Your recesses he'll cease to explore;
For mineral veins and organic remains
    No Stratum again will he bore.

Oh! his Wit shone like Crystal! his knowledge profound
    From Gravel to Granite descended;
No Trap could deceive him, no Slip could confound,
    Nor specimen true or pretended.
He knew the birth-rock of each pebble so round
    And how far its tour had extended.

His eloquence roll'd like the Deluge retiring
    Which Mastodon carcases floated;
To a subject obscure he gave charms so inspiring
    Young and Old on Geology doated.
He stood forth like an Outlier; his hearers admiring
    In pencil each anecdote noted.

Where shall we our great Professor inter,
    That in peace may rest his bones?
If we hew him a rocky sepulchre

He'll rise and break the stones,
And examine each Stratum that lies around,
For he's quite in his element under ground.

If with Mattock and Spade his body we lay
    In the common alluvial soil,
He'll start up and snatch those tools away
    Of his own Geological toil.
In a Stratum so young the Professor disdains
That embedded should be his Organic Remains.

Then expos'd to the drip of some case-hard'ning spring,
    His carcase let Stalactite cover,
And to Oxford the petrified sage let us bring,
    When he is incrusted all over;
There 'mid Mammoths and Crocodiles, high on a Shelf,
Let him stand as a Monument raised to himself.

Australia's first victory over England in Test cricket on English soil in 1882 astonished English fans and resulted in the following mock obituary by the *Sporting Times* journalist, Reginald Shirley Brooks. The 'obituary' ultimately gave rise to the name 'The Ashes', by which the Test cricket series played regularly between England and Australia is known.

In affectionate Remembrance

of

ENGLISH CRICKET

WHICH DIED AT THE OVAL,

on

29th August, 1882,

Deeply lamented by a large circle of sorrowing
friends and acquaintances,

R.I.P.

NB the body will be cremated and the
ashes taken to Australia

Winston Churchill's (1874–1965) suggested epitaph on himself.

am ready to meet my Maker. Whether my Maker is prepared for the great rdeal of meeting me is another matter.

Saadat Hasan Manto's (1912–55) suggested epitaph for himself, composed six months before his death.

Iere lies Saadat Hasan Manto and with him lie buried all the secrets and nysteries of the art of short-story writing. Under tons of earth he lies, still vondering who among the two is the greater short-story writer: God or he.

In the first decades of the twentieth century, celebrities were invited by magazines to suggest their own epitaphs, giving rise to a vogue.

lka Chas (1900–78): 'I've finally gotten to the bottom of things.'

ing Crosby (1903–77): 'He was an average guy who could carry a tune.'

V.C. Fields (1880–1946): 'On the whole, I'd rather be in Philadelphia.'

Jeorge Gershwin (1898–1937): 'Here lies the body of George Gershwin, merican composer. American? Composer?'

Jroucho Marx (1890–1977): 'Here lies Groucho Marx – and lies and lies nd lies. PS. He never kissed an ugly girl.'

rnest Hemmingway (1899–1961): 'Pardon me for not getting up.'

lfred Hitchcock (1899–1980): 'I'm involved in a plot.'

Jerald S. Kaufman: 'Over my dead body.'

Hilaire Belloc's (1870-1953) suggested epitaph for himself.

> When I am dead, I hope it may be said:
> 'His sins were scarlet, but his books were read'.

From the poem 'C.M.B.', by Sir John Sparrow (1906–92), the Warden of All Souls, Oxford, on his friend Sir Maurice Bowra (1898–1971).

Send us to Hell or Heaven or where you will,
Promise us only you'll be with us still:
Without you, Heaven would be too dull to bear,
And Hell will not be Hell if you are there.

Bibliography

Allen, Thomas, *The History and Antiquities of London, Westminster, Southwark, and Parts Adjacent* (London, 1827–1829).

Andrews, William, *Curious Epitaphs*, 2nd edn (London, 1899).

Bailey, Brian (ed.), *Aubrey's Brief Lives* (Harmondsworth, 1949, rpt 1972).

Baines, Edward, *History of the County Palatine and Duchy of Lancaster* (London, 1836).

Bartlett, William Abraham, *The History and Antiquities of the Parish of Wimbledon, Surrey* (London, 1865).

Blomefield, Francis and Charles Parkin, *An Essay towards a Topographical History of the County of Norfolk*, 2nd edn (1805–1810).

Bowden, John, *The Epitaph Writer, Consisting of Six Hundred Original Epitaphs, Moral, Admonitory, Humorous and Satirical...* (Chester, 1791).

British History Online (www.british-history.ac.uk).

Chalmers, Alexander, *The General Biographical Dictionary* (London, 1812–1817).

Clarkson, Christopher, *The History of Richmond, in the County of York* (Richmond, 1814).

Clifford, Eileen, *Cambridgeshire Epitaphs*, Cambridgeshire Historical Trust (Little Gidding, 1993).

Colonial Graves' (colonialgraves.tumblr.com).

Costin, Diana, *Grave Tales from Berkshire* (Seaford, 1999).

Fairley, William *Epitaphiana; Or, The Curiosities of Churchyard Literature* (London, 1873).

Faulkner, Thomas, *The History and Antiquities of the Parish of Hammersmith* (London, 1839).

Find A Grave' (findagrave.com).

The History of Northampton and its Vicinity, Brought Down to the Present Time (Northampton, 1815).

Hughson, David, *London, Being an Accurate History and Description of th British Metropolis and its Neighbourhood ...*, 5 vols (1805–1813).

Jervise, Andrew, *Epitaphs and Inscriptions from Burial Grounds and Ol Buildings in the North-east of Scotland* (Edinburgh, 1875).

Le Neve, John, *Monumenta Anglicana* (London, 1718).

Love, Dane, *Scottish Kirkyards* (London, 1989).

Mackail, J.W., *Select Epigrams from the Greek Anthology* (London and Nev York, 1906).

Maiben, Frederick, *An Original Collection of Extant Epitaphs* (London, 1870

Mann, Thomas C. and Janet Greene, *Over their Dead Bodies: Yankee Epitapl and History* (Brattleboro, VT, 1962).

National Maritime Museum, Maritime Memorials, (blogarchive.rmg.co.uk memorials).

Norfolk, Horatio Edward, *Gleanings in Graveyards: A Collection of Curiou Epitaphs* (London, 1866).

Orchard, Robert, *A New Select Collection of Epitaphs* (London, 1827).

Parker, John, *Reading Latin Epitaphs: A Handbook for Beginners wit Illustrations* (Exeter, 2012).

'People and Places in Kirkcudbrightshire' (www.kirkyards.co.uk).

Perkins, Frank Herman, *Handbook of Old Burial Hill, Plymouth, Massachuset* (Plymouth, MA, 1902).

Pettigrew, T.J., *Chronicles of the Tombs: A Select Collection of Epitapl* (London, 1878).

Potter, T.F., *North Country Epitaphs* (Clapham, 1979).

Public Monuments and Sculptural Association (www.pmsa.org.uk).

Ravenshaw, Thomas FitzArthur, *Antiente Epitaphes (from A.D. 1250 to A.L 1800)* (London, 1878).

Recording Archive for Public Sculpture in Norfolk and Suffolk (www.racns co.uk).

Rees, Nigel, *EPITAPHS: A Dictionary of Grave Epigrams and Memoric Eloquence* (London, 1993).

Roffe, Edwin, *British Monumental Inscriptions: Gathered Occasionally, fror Divers Churchyards* (London, 1859).

Rogers, Charles, *Monuments and Monumental Inscriptions in Scotland*, 2 vol (London, 1871).

Rudder, Samuel, *The History and Antiquities of Gloucester* (Cirencester, 1781).

The Soldier's Companion; Or, Martial Recorder, vol. 1 (London, 1824).

Stabb, J., *Some Old Devon Churches, Their Rood Screens, Pulpits, Fonts, etc.* (London, 1908–1911).

Thoroton, Robert, *Thornton's History of Nottinghamshire*, vol. 1 (London, 1797).

Toldervy, W., *Select Epitaphs*, 2 vols [in 1] (London, 1775).

A Tour on the Banks of the Thames from London to Oxford, in the Autumn of 1829. By a Pedestrian (London, 1834).

Transactions of the Historical Society of Leicestershire and Cheshire, for the Year 1899, v. 51, N.S., vol. 15.

Transactions of the Thoroton Society of Nottinghamshire (1898–).

Unusual Epitaphs' (www.roys-roy.blogspot.co.uk/2014/01/unusual-epitaphs. html).

Utechin, Patricia, *Epitaphs from Oxfordshire Churches*, 2nd edn (Oxford, 1990).

Warmington, E.H., *Remains of Old Latin, Volume 4: Archaic Inscriptions*, Loeb Classical Library (Cambridge, MA, and London, 1940).

Weever, John, *Ancient Fvnerall Monvments* (London, 1631).

Weller, Michael, *Devon Epitaphs* (Wellington, 2010).

West, William, *The History, Topography and Directory of Warwickshire* (Birmingham, 1830).

Westminster Abbey (www.westminster-abbey.org/our-history/people).

Willsher, Betty, *Scottish Epitaphs: Epitaphs and Images from Scottish Graveyards* (Edinburgh, 1996).

Wilson, David M., *Awful Ends: The British Museum Book of Epitaphs* (London, 1992).

Wright, Geoffrey N., *Discovering Epitaphs* (Princes Risborough, 1972, rpt. 1990).

Index